Simple
Menus for
the Bento
Box

Ellen Greaves and Wayne Nish

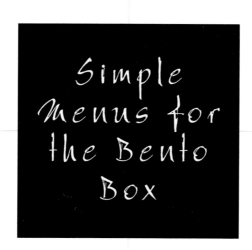

Simple
Menus for
the Bento
Box

Photography by
Wayne Nish

William Morrow and Company, Inc., New York

Library of Congress Cataloging-in-Publication Data

Greaves, Ellen.
Simple menus for the bento box / Ellen Greaves & Wayne Nish.—1st ed.
p.   cm.
Includes bibliographical references and index.
ISBN 0-688-14204-4
1. Cookery, American.   2. Food presentation.
3. Table setting and decoration.
I. Nish, Wayne.   II. Title.
TX715.G811465   1998
641.5973—DC21   97–31929
CIP

Printed in Singapore

First Edition

1   2   3   4   5   6   7   8   9   10

BOOK DESIGN BY RICHARD ORIOLO

www.williammorrow.com

Dedication
and Acknowledgments

We would like to dedicate this book to the late Fred Bridge. The seed of this book was planted when we were guests of Mr. Bridge at a party in the Waldorf-Astoria in honor of Craig Claiborne.

This book is intended as a primer on simple cooking presented in a beautiful and unique manner. It began as a natural addition to the work that Ellen has been doing as chef at The Tea Box Café at Takashimaya in New York City, and that Wayne has become well known for at his restaurant March, where his personal interpretation of a new American cuisine is found in a multicultural and globally influenced menu.

The restaurant project that was to become The Tea Box was originally conceived of by consultant Gary A. Goldberg, executive director of the Culinary Arts Program at The New School. He was assisted by Elizabeth Andoh, the Japanese cookbook author and a recognized expert on Japanese food culture.

The central idea for the restaurant concept was to be an East-West food style reflecting the philosophy of Takashimaya's new flagship store on Fifth Avenue, the best of both cultures. In seeking an executive chef for the project, Gary approached Wayne, who recommended Ellen. We had originally started to work together at The Quilted Giraffe in the 1980s. At that time a Japanese influence to a newly emerging style of New American cuisine was gaining fame. We had also both worked on tiered bentos for lunch service at The Quilted Giraffe. And Gary and Elizabeth's original plans emphasized a shokado bento as a vehicle for daily specials at The Tea Box.

Stylistically, this book is the direct result of applying strong visual graphics of a shokado bento box to a photographic presentation. Of course, many people contributed to the ideas and production of it.

We wrote all of the recipes together. Ellen prepared all of the food to be recipe tested and photographed. Wayne was the photographer and did the food styling. Jeff Derouen, then a student extern at March restaurant, was enlisted as photo assistant.

Wayne is deeply indebted to Tom Kirkman, friend and photography mentor, without whose teaching and guidance he would not have been able to tackle a professional project of this scope.

Peter Frank was invaluable as prop stylist and made numerous successful suggestions for plateware and table accessory combinations. He was able to source an endless supply of beautiful dishes in the tiny sizes necessary for the bento boxes we had found, and made appropriate choices as solutions for when the reader has problems finding porcelain intended for such use. Glass and ceramic tiles, agate coasters, tiny flowerpot liners, live or dried leaves, and beautiful papers cut to size were all pressed into service as substitutions for traditional Japanese dinnerware. The only restrictions were that they be 3 1/2 inches or smaller in diameter and beautiful to look at. Peter was also brilliant at locating exotic papers, wonderful fabrics, and other materials that were used as backgrounds.

Marion Johnson at Designs by Marion supplied some of the most beautiful pieces we were able to use for the photo shoots. Her store, located on the same block as March restaurant, has one of the most complete selections of Western table accoutrements in New York.

David Nussbaum's literary help and support was invaluable. A series of editors, Ann

Bramson, Kathleen Hackett, and Gail Kinn, each made their own contributions, but Justin Schwartz finally brought it to completion.

The obvious format for the photograph was square, to mirror the image of the shokado bento box. So we naturally chose a 2¼-inch medium format. Tom's expert advice resulted in our using the following set-up:

The camera was Hasselblad 500CM equipped with a PM-5 prism finder. Lenses used were the Carl Zeiss 120 mm/f4 Macro-Planar and the 60 mm/f3.5 Distagon, both used with extension tubes when needed. A Hasselblad Polaroid back was used for proofing with Polaroid Pro-Vivid film, and all chromes were made with Fuji Provia RDPII.

A single Balcar Starflash power pack with 2 interdependent channels was used to power one Balcar U-Head up above as a fill light through a white screen and one adjustable focus Balcar Z-Head fitted with a Balcar Opalite served as the main horizontal light source. Only changing the distance of the two light sources created the diversity needed to properly light the subjects. A soft gold reflector completed the lighting tasks by filling in front and side shadows.

Carol Color Labs in New York City did all of the film processing.

Contents

Introduction

Opening the Shokado Bento

More than three hundred years ago, a Japanese Buddhist priest adapted a common farmer's seed box—a wooden box with four compartments—to hold his painting supplies. The priest, one of the most famous painters and calligraphers of his era, created his art in a small thatched hut, a retreat he named Shokado, or "Pine Blossom Hall."

Many years later, in the early part of the twentieth century, an inventive Japanese cook found another use for the box: as a container in which to serve a meal with four dishes. He called this box shokado, recalling the priest and his art, and it quickly became one of the most popular forms of bento, or "boxed meal." The lacquered box, covered with a lid, is today a common sight at lunch, dinner, and party tables in Japan.

In our American kitchens over the past decade, we have adapted the shokado box yet again. We use it as a simple device to serve everyday meals with artfulness and ceremony—to show off the natural beauty of food and to heighten the drama of culinary presentation.

The effect of the shokado box is powerful. Set before each guest—its plain lid hiding a carefully composed feast of small dishes—the box is both curtain and stage. Uncovered, it reveals a tableau of color, form, line, and texture (and a tantalizing burst of aroma). And it is the set for an exciting play of flavors and textures: four distinctive dishes, savored separately and together, displaying the harmony and counterpoint of a great meal.

How to Use This Book

Creating a meal in a bento box is a unique culinary experience, offering pleasure on many levels: in cooking, in visual design, in service, and, of course, in eating. We have written this book to bring these pleasures to anyone who loves delicious food beautifully served, whatever your level of kitchen expertise. Guided by the menus, recipes, and pictures you will find in these pages, you can easily create a bento meal—one with a flavor and a look that is distinctly your own.

We have created twelve menus—three for each season, each with four component dishes—specifically for the shokado bento box. These are foods that we love—cooked with the care we've learned from years in the kitchen—but you don't have to be a professional chef to make them. Our recipes are quick and simple, and we tell you how to produce the shape, color, and texture of the food that is best for each presentation.

Nor do you have to be a professional food stylist to create an eye-opening bento. You will find in the menu headnotes and the recipes (and of course in the pictures) our suggestions for garnishing, plating, and assembling a gorgeous visual composition. (With just a few exceptions, all of the recipes in this book can be completed well ahead of mealtime. You will have plenty of time to assemble foods and plates in a beautiful fashion.)

To be sure, we encourage you to fully enjoy bento cookery: to acquire bento boxes and dishes, and to prepare a complete bento menu. But the recipes in this book will taste delicious whether eaten from a bento box or not. You can prepare a dish all by itself or serve it with others of your choosing and find full, satisfying flavor.

Similarly, the dishes will look beautiful even outside a bento box. As you see in the individual pictures, you can create a design of food, plates, mats, tablecloths, and other accessories that will make a pleasing composition and capture the diner's attention.

However you choose to use the recipes and information here, we hope you will enjoy a wonderful lesson we have learned through bento cookery: The simple exercise of care is the key to realizing the potential of each dish and of the whole shokado bento box. Take care as you cut your vegetables, care as you choose the plates, and care as you assemble and arrange the meal before you consider it perfect.

Your care will be expressed in the unique beauty and flavor of your creation. Through your artful effort, you can transform the simple bento box into a treasure chest for every person at your table.

Putting Food in the Painter's Box

Pay attention to the food: That is every cook and chef's silent wish. Without diminishing the spontaneity of an occasion or distracting the course of conversation, we all want our guests to *notice* what we serve them.

In this regard, the shokado bento box is an aesthetic device of enormous power. Its stark grid creates an ordered space that focuses the eye upon the meal with great clarity. Each compartment—uniform in size—becomes a showcase for the dish within, carefully displayed on a unique pedestal. Each stands out against the black lacquer backdrop. Yet within the frame as a whole, the four components become a dynamic composition, an interactivity of line, shape, and color.

The bento box commands attention for the food, as the components of a meal are at once linked—yet separated—in an exciting tension that exceeds the possibilities of a single plate.

Eating a Bento Meal

In our bentos, there are no designated "main" dishes or "side" dishes. Balanced, all in moderate portions, no dish is more important than another. This may seem exotic to the diner. Our guests will sometimes ask, "What do I eat first?" Our answer: "Anything you like." With four tempting places to start, the bento box gives them the freedom to control their own tasting experience.

Here is a wonderful challenge to the chef. In most cooking, we can subtly control the tasting experience of others. Through the service of sequential courses—by designating appetizers, first courses, and main courses—we can focus the diner's attention exclusively on each of a series of dishes that showcase particular flavors and textures. This is a cumulative, linear unfolding of a dinner's drama.

But it is different when we serve four distinctive dishes in a bento box. Side by side, there are flavor experiences of every kind. Now, each dish must have its own integrity of taste and texture, yet must be perfectly compatible with all the others. In whatever manner they are tasted—whether all the soup is carefully sipped or the meat is devoured at once, or whether every dish is sampled in a rambling, leisurely manner—each mouthful must be satisfying and interesting, and go well with whatever comes next.

Creating a Book of Bentos

This book explores the presentational power of the shokado bento—yet we did not begin with visual ideas. We started, as we always do, with foods and flavors. Over the course of a year we developed menus of interesting dishes—combinations of the familiar and the exotic—that taste marvelous when served together.

We discovered what the boxes would look like only when we cooked each meal. As we do in our restaurants, we designed the presentations spontaneously. We gathered a collection of bento wares, including three distinct shokado boxes, and over a hundred different serving vessels: dishes, plates, bowls, shells, leaves, blocks, and mats. As each menu was prepared, we put food, dishes, and boxes together.

We sought interesting juxtapositions of color and shape, sometimes trying several different plates for a recipe. We changed the arrangement of dishes in the box, we rearranged the food on the plates, until we found the composition that best pleased the eye and tempted the palate.

Then we took the photographs you see in this book. This part of our project had two purposes: As chefs, we wanted to use photography itself as a presentational form, a medium to show the natural beauty of food, serving utensils, and the visual effect of the bento frame. We also wanted to capture the moment that the dishes came together, as we would serve them to our guests—not as they would be styled just for a photo. We wanted to preserve the composition that we were inspired to find as we cooked and assembled.

Putting Together a Bento Service

Your first bento project (for which no cooking is necessary) should be the gathering of a shokado bento service for use at your table. This can be an enjoyable exploration in itself, as finding the boxes may take you to marvelous Asian markets and import stores. And, as we have found, assembling an eclectic set of dishes to go into the bentos is an ongoing treasure hunt. Some bentos are sold with a basic set of dishes, which is fine to get you started, but you may find yourself combing antiques shops, kitchenware stores, flea markets, and craft shops on all your travels, seeking the perfect, diminutive plate or bowl that will bring an exciting new look to your bento meal.

The box must be your first acquisition—don't start to collect plates until you know the exact dimensions of the compartments. (Most shokado boxes are approximately ten-inch squares, and dishes must have diameters of about four inches or less.) Shokado boxes are sold at larger Oriental kitchenware stores in many American cities and can be ordered by mail from the suppliers listed on page 152. Prices for the common plastic boxes can be as little as ten dollars, and elaborate antique shokado boxes can sell for several thousand dollars.

As you can see from our pictures, there is no limit, other than size, to the kind of vessel that can work well in a bento box. Shapes, colors, patterns, and materials *should* vary as much as possible. Make sure that your basic collection includes rounds, ovals, squares, triangles, flat, and bowl-shaped items. Look especially for dishes that give linearity to the box through shape or pattern. Have an assortment of modern and antique dishes; mix stark and baroque patterns. Some of the most useful colors that we like are hues of blue and earth tones, such as greens and browns. You will be delighted to find that food also goes wonderfully on shades of mauve and purple.

Of course, you want to be certain that everything you use is safe for serving food. Be cautious about what you place on unglazed pottery. And if you are going to use plant leaves as a platform—which we do with wonderful effect—be certain that they are nontoxic (and from a plant that hasn't been sprayed).

A Note on Ingredients

The recipes in this book are exceedingly simple—simple to make and simple to shop for. If you are unfamiliar with an ingredient, please try to make an effort to find it. You might just find something new that you like. And if you make it a new part of your pantry inventory, we will be happy you did.

Spices like whole coriander or mustard seeds are sold by the major spice brands in most supermarket chains. It might seem excessive to buy a jar when just a teaspoon is called for in a given recipe, but it's worth the expense. You can also find these spices in Indian markets and where canning or pickling supplies are sold.

Extra-virgin olive oil was once an exotic and expensive ingredient. It isn't so exotic anymore and prices are coming down as competition increases for an enlarged market demand. The difference in flavor from regular or blended oils is inestimable. Don't be tempted by lesser substitutions.

Dry white vermouth is a fortified wine that has a richness of flavor not found in many dry white wines. It provides a gentle and sweet nuance yet at the same time offers a complexity that makes building layers of flavors possible when creating a dish. It is also a consistent product that will always achieve the same results for you. The French brands are the ones we prefer, although the Italian brands will also give you good results. Medium-body, dry, and semidry white wines can be substituted when desired, but know that a different result will appear.

All salts are not created equal. Iodized table salt is the cheapest in cost and harshest in flavor. Kosher salt should be the standard in your kitchen as it contains no additives and dissolves easily and quickly. It also has a bright, clean flavor. Natural sea salts top the list for best flavor. Many are harvested and processed throughout the world. Some of the best we have encountered are the ones from Brittany in France or Japan, but we have tasted good ones from Italy and Korea too.

Many of our recipes call for chicken stock. There are two reasons for this. One is that it has a neutral flavor that will accommodate many different foods. The other is convenience. It is inexpensive and easy to make and freeze for future use. It is also commonly available canned. Some of the national brands are quite good and could be used in a pinch. Just be sure to look for the lower-sodium type. This will allow you to reduce the stock more without intensifying the salt level too much. Vegetable broth can be substituted in many cases, but the results will be different from what we intended. If the vegetable broth contains tomato, it will change the color of the dish as well.

The big lesson here is that good cooking can be only as good as the ingredients you use. No amount of technique can cover for mediocre or less than excellent ingredients. Buy the best you can, treat them as simply as possible, and the result will be good.

All of the recipes are written to yield 4 bento portions. Four bento portions equal 4 appetizer portions or 2 entree portions.

Spring

Roast Cornish Hen

Potato Salad with Olives and Walnuts

Baby Artichokes
with Coriander and Thyme

Japanese Rice with
Hard-Boiled Eggs and Chives

Sporting a sunny flower blossom shape of rice, this bento is perfect for a spring or early summer day: a simple, light and satisfying meal, showing off the sprightly flavors of its seasonal components. A few presentational touches demonstrate how easy it is to create a gorgeous display of food's natural beauty.

Everything can be prepared well in advance of serving and you will have plenty of time to indulge in the art of bento plating and assembly. Simmer baby artichokes with lemon, thyme, and coriander seeds and cool. Roast small Cornish hens until deeply colored.

Enrich cooked Japanese rice with hard-boiled eggs. Last, but in no hurry, toss together the potato salad.

The salad, indeed, is a perfect example of our approach to balancing flavors in our bento dishes. An utterly simple mix of select ingredients, in proper proportions, it provides a wonderfully complex flavor experience. You may use chopsticks or a fork, but make sure you taste a walnut, a couple of pieces of potato, an olive, and a chervil sprig at the same time!

Plating the dishes also calls for nothing more complicated than careful attention. Quartered baby artichokes are naturally beautiful: With no choke, the inside displays a delicate contrast of color, the outside a lovely curve; the sharp point of the quarter provides a sculptural accent. A simple pile of slices, thoughtfully placed, can reveal all these facets. In our bento, curve and color are highlighted by the plate's rim with its streaks of matching and contrasting color. Dots of whole coriander seed add detail and taste great too!

The similarly proportioned pile of roast chicken also benefits from the exercise of care: We chose the prettiest side of each cut-up piece and made sure that was the one that showed. Take a moment with any piece of food and select its best-looking side for presentation.

Of course, attention is drawn immediately to the bright dish of rice, shaped like a cherry blossom (with its bits of egg further suggesting the floral colors of daffodil and daisy). As easy as it is lovely, this can be shaped with a rice press or simply molded with a cup and a chopstick, as our recipe describes.

A note on overall design: We used just a few lines, created by the food and dishes, to draw the eye down and across the box. The axis of drumstick and chopsticks, the slats of the bamboo weave on which the rice is served, and even the delicate diagonal of the chive garnish help to bring this bento together visually. Lines like these will emerge in every shokado presentation: It's the chef's prerogative—and pleasure—to arrange them in a pleasing way.

Roast Cornish Hen

2 Cornish hens (or baby chickens under 1 pound)
2 tablespoons extra-virgin olive oil
Salt and freshly ground black pepper

Preheat the oven to 450°F.

Rub the hens all over with the oil, then season to taste with the salt and pepper. Place the hens in a large roasting pan, breast side up. Place in the oven and roast for 45 minutes. Remove the pan from the oven, move the hens to a cutting board, and let rest for 15 minutes. Using a sharp knife, carve each breast off the bone. Cut the wings at the joint, leaving one section of wing attached to the breast. Cut the legs from the birds and separate the drumstick from the thigh.

ASSEMBLY

Serve half a hen per person. Make a base with the breast pieces, then finish with the leg and use the wing to balance the drumstick. We chose a cool blue plate that contrasted with the warm tawny color of the chicken skin.

Potato Salad with Olives and Walnuts

½ pound tiny whole potatoes or 4 small yellow potatoes, preferably Yukon Gold, cut into 1-inch pieces

2 tablespoons sherry vinegar or good-quality white wine vinegar

⅓ cup pitted oil-cured black olives

⅔ cup walnut pieces

⅓ cup extra-virgin olive oil

Salt and freshly ground black pepper

Fresh chervil and tarragon sprigs

Fill a 6-cup saucepan with lightly salted water and place over high heat. Bring to a boil, then add the potatoes and cook until tender when pierced with a knife, about 15 minutes. Drain immediately. Place the potatoes in a bowl, sprinkle with vinegar, and let cool. Toss with the olives, walnuts, and olive oil and season to taste with salt and pepper.

ASSEMBLY

Place in small, cup-shaped bowls making the pile as high as possible, choosing and placing the top pieces with care. Garnish with the chervil and tarragon sprigs.

Baby Artichokes with Coriander and Thyme

Makes 4 bento servings

8 baby artichokes, no larger than 1½ inches in diameter

1 medium lemon, halved crosswise

1 head garlic, halved crosswise

3 sprigs fresh thyme, or 1 teaspoon dried

1 tablespoon whole coriander seeds

1 tablespoon salt

To trim the artichokes, leave the stem on and peel. Cut away the tough outer layer of leaves. Cut off the top third of the artichokes and discard. Rub the artichokes with the lemon to keep them from turning brown, then cut each lemon half into quarters.

Place the artichokes, lemon wedges, garlic, thyme, coriander seeds, and salt in a pot just large enough to hold the artichokes in one layer. Add ½ inch of water. Lay a piece of parchment paper on top of the artichokes to keep them moist. Place the pot over medium-high heat and bring to a simmer. Reduce the heat to low and simmer the artichokes until there is no resistance when the artichokes are pierced with a small knife, 20 to 25 minutes. Remove the pot from the heat and let the artichokes cool in their liquid. When the artichokes are cool, cut them into quarters and discard the liquid.

ASSEMBLY

Choose a flat dish or plate to show off the height of this recipe and build the artichokes into a tall pile. The quarters have different faces with different colors—yellow at the center, then pale green and then darker gray-green toward the outside—and different textures. Serve the artichokes at room temperature for the most flavor.

Japanese Rice with Hard-Boiled Eggs and Chives

Makes 4 bento servings

2 cups Japanese rice (see Note)

2 extra large eggs

Kosher salt

1 tablespoon peanut oil

Freshly ground black pepper

1 tablespoon finely chopped chives

Lightly rinse the rice in a sieve until all the rice is wet. Put it in a 6-cup saucepan with 2 cups water and let it soak for 30 minutes.

Meanwhile, put the eggs in a small pot with enough water to cover. Bring the water to a boil over high heat, reduce the heat to low, and simmer for 11 minutes. Cool the eggs under cold running water and peel. If they are difficult to peel, crack the shells lightly and let the eggs sit in a bowl of water for 5 minutes. Separate the egg whites from the yolks. Finely chop the whites and lightly crumble the yolks.

Once the rice has soaked, stir it well and place the pan over high heat. Add 1 teaspoon salt and let the rice come to a boil. Stir it again and turn the heat down as low as possible. Cover the saucepan with a tight-fitting lid and simmer for 11 minutes. Remove the rice from the heat and let it sit, covered, for 5 minutes.

Transfer the rice to a bowl and stir it well, using a flat spatula or a wooden spoon and stirring with a folding motion. This motion, used in Japan, does not crush the rice, but mixes and cools it. Let the rice cool for 10 minutes, or until it is lukewarm. Stir in the chopped egg whites and the peanut oil and season to taste with salt and pepper. Add the egg yolks after the rice is mixed and seasoned, so that the egg yolks remain distinct dots of yellow. Stir in the egg yolks just enough to mix them in. If the yolks are overmixed, the rice turns yellow.

A S S E M B L Y

To shape the rice, line a coffee cup with plastic wrap, fill it with 1 inch of rice, then twist the plastic wrap closed and press down. This forces the rice into the bottom of the cup and gives a 1-inch disk of rice.

Use a chopstick or other pointed object to make 5 equidistant indentations into the edges of the disk. This forms the plain disk of rice into a flower shape. Unwrap the plastic and place the rice on a plate that contrasts the shape or texture of the rice. Here, we used a square bamboo mat with a strong vertical direction to contrast the roundness of the rice and sprinkled a line of chopped chives diagonally across the rice to emphasize the square shape of the mat.

N O T E   This is a short-grained rice that is sticky when it is cooked. We use Kokuho Rose, a rice grown in California. Japanese rice is available in Korean delis and many supermarkets.

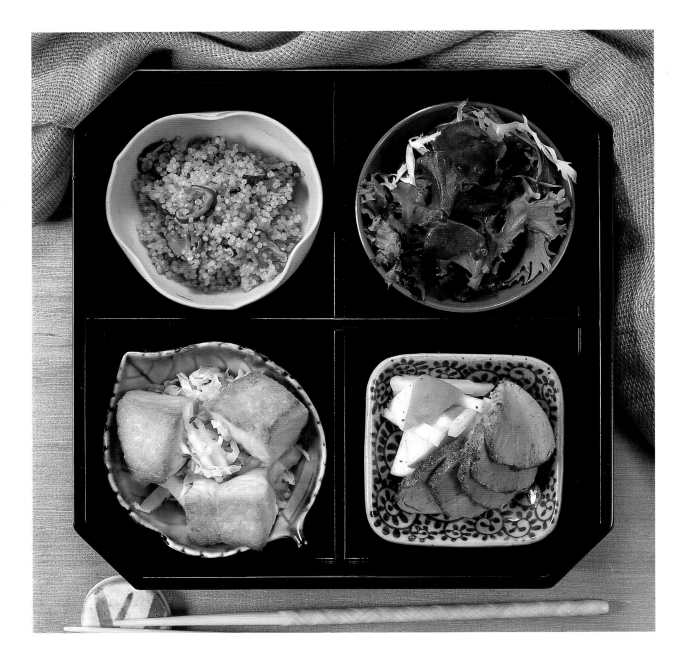

Spice-Crusted Pork Tenderloin with Apple and Kohlrabi

Quinoa with Black Mushrooms

Seared Salmon on Napa Cabbage

Mesclun Salad

here to start eating this delicious, multitextured bento of subtle and distinctive contrasts?

We are of two minds. The mesclun salad, with sweet, bitter, and spicy lettuces accented with champagne vinegar, is a lively place to begin. Yet it is also a perfect light note on which to finish, after enjoying the weightier substance and dramatic contrasts of the other dishes.

There's a great interplay between the seared salmon—creamy, rich, and unctuous—

and its bed of still-crunchy Napa cabbage slivers, warm and lightly acidic from simmering in white wine, spiced with caraway and mustard seed. (We urge you to buy fat and luscious Norwegian salmon. Patiently let it sear well on its top side and serve it while still rare and moist.)

Move to another sensual contrast: the heat and spice of pork tenderloin slices—crusted with cumin, cinnamon, and black pepper—matched with cool, crunchy wedges of apple and lemony, raw kohlrabi. We love the color contrast of the cool, green Granny apple skin with the warm pork slices and the contrast between the acute angles of the apple chunks with the right angles and thinner lines of the kohlrabi julienne.

Combine these with the quinoa, the marvelously nutritious grain of the Andes, its nutty taste deepened with slivers of dried shiitake mushroom.

The flavors here benefit from bold contrast, yet the box also reveals that minimal contrast can have a dramatic visual effect. We deliberately chose a gold and brown bowl for the gold and brown quinoa-mushroom mix. The golden flecks in the bowl and grain play off each other—and increase the radiance of the dish. Don't be locked into the commonplace notion that food colors must always be set off by contrast—you may heighten the impact through a display of similar colors.

We were happy to have a multitude of small dish shapes to choose from, and this bento shows the wonderful effect of dish variety. The lobed bowl of quinoa, the square plate, and the leaf plate provide not only variety but a strong and dynamic axis in the frame. Even if your selection is limited, don't always choose round plates.

Some observations: We like odd numbers. We would not plate four chunks of salmon or four slices of pork. And we enjoy the dimension of verticality that comes from draping the pork slices against a pile of apple and kohlrabi.

Spice-Crusted Pork Tenderloin
with Apple and Kohlrabi

Makes 4 bento servings

1 tablespoon ground cumin

¼ teaspoon ground cinnamon

Freshly ground black pepper

¾ pound pork tenderloin, trimmed of fat and silverskin

Kosher salt

2 tablespoons peanut oil

1 tart apple, preferably Granny Smith

1 bulb kohlrabi, peeled (see Note)

1 tablespoon fresh lemon juice

Preheat the oven to 450°F.

Mix the cumin, cinnamon, and ½ teaspoon pepper on a flat plate that is as long as the tenderloin.

Season the pork tenderloin with salt, then roll it in the spice powder mix to coat the tenderloin evenly. Heat an ovenproof sauté pan over medium heat, add the peanut oil, and allow it to heat for 15 seconds.

Sauté the tenderloin in the hot oil, turning approximately every minute until each of the 4 sides has a crisp, brown velvety crust. Finish cooking in the oven for 7 minutes, or until the pork has an internal temperature of 140°F or is just slightly pink. Let the pork rest for 10 minutes.

continued

Spring

Cut the apple into quarters, core it, and cut each quarter into angular chunks ½ inch across. (See Note on chunk cutting, below.) Cut the kohlrabi into julienne sticks by cutting the bulb into ¼-inch slices, then cutting across into ¼-inch sticks. Toss the apple and kohlrabi pieces with the lemon juice, salt, and pepper.

A S S E M B L Y

Mound the apple and kohlrabi on plates. Using a very sharp knife, slice the pork tenderloin straight across the grain into ¼-inch slices. Drape these slices over the salad, fanning them to have a focal point on the salad to show the pretty pink of the interior.

N O T E   If kohlrabi is unavailable, substitute fennel bulb or celery root.

Note about chunk cuts: We like chunks to be all the same size, bite size, but to have many different angles showing. We love this cut because it is much simpler to cut than dice or cubes, looks less rigid, and gives a controlled anarchy of angles.

Quinoa with Black Mushrooms

Makes 4 bento servings

¼ cup dried sliced shiitake mushrooms, or 4 whole dried shiitake caps or 4 fresh
    shiitake caps

1 cup quinoa

Salt to taste

If using dried mushrooms, rehydrate them by pouring boiling water over them to cover in a bowl. Let sit until soft, about 10 minutes for sliced mushrooms, 30 minutes for whole ones. Lift the mushrooms out of the water, leaving any sediment behind. If using dried whole caps, use a very sharp knife to slice them across the cap into ⅛-inch slices. If using fresh mushrooms, remove the stems and slice the caps into ⅛-inch slices.

Rinse the quinoa in a fine strainer under running water until the water runs clear. Place a dry 6-cup saucepan over medium heat for 2 minutes. Add the wet quinoa and stir it until it is dry and a little darker and starts to smell toasted, approximately 4 minutes.

Bring 2 cups water to a boil and pour over the quinoa with the salt and mushrooms. Raise the heat under the quinoa to high and bring back to a boil. Then cover, turn the heat to low, and simmer for 15 minutes. Remove from the heat and let it rest, covered, for 5 to 10 minutes. Fluff it with a fork to separate the grains and stop the cooking.

ASSEMBLY

We chose a deep gold-colored bowl for the grain to accent the natural tawny color of the quinoa. Pile it to get some height and make sure the pretty curve of a few mushrooms shows.

Spring

Seared Salmon on Napa Cabbage

1 small head of Napa cabbage

½ cup dry, full-flavored white wine

1 tablespoon whole caraway seeds (or fennel or anise seeds)

1 teaspoon whole yellow mustard seeds (or black or brown)

Salt and freshly ground black pepper

12 ounces salmon fillet, preferably Norwegian

2 tablespoons extra-virgin olive oil

Cut the Napa cabbage in quarters. Cut out the core from each piece, then slice across into ¼-inch slivers.

Place the white wine, caraway seeds, and mustard seeds in a 6-cup saucepan and bring to a boil over high heat. Add the cabbage and season to taste with salt and pepper. Reduce the heat to medium-low and let simmer for 2 minutes, stirring well. Cover and let simmer until tender, about 5 minutes more. Adjust the seasoning, remove from the heat, and cover to keep warm.

Cut the salmon into bite-size cubes about 1 inch across and season to taste with salt and pepper. Heat a sauté pan over high heat, add the oil, and let heat for 15 seconds. Add the salmon cubes to the pan and sauté on one side only until golden brown, about 1 minute. Let cook until you see the edges start to look brown, then lift a piece to check if it really is evenly browned on the bottom.

ASSEMBLY

Mound the cabbage in the center of a deep plate, leaving some empty space around the edge to show off the plate. Arrange the salmon cubes, browned side up, on the cabbage.

Mesclun Salad

Makes 4 bento servings

2 cups mesclun salad mix

1 teaspoon light brown sugar

¾ tablespoon champagne vinegar or good-quality white wine vinegar

½ teaspoon kosher or sea salt

¼ teaspoon freshly ground black pepper

2 tablespoons extra-virgin olive oil

Wash the mesclun mix and pick it over. Dry the leaves very well. In a mixing bowl, whisk together the brown sugar, vinegar, salt, and pepper. Whisk in the olive oil in a fine stream, then taste and correct the seasoning. Toss the lettuce well with the dressing to coat each bit with a very fine layer of dressing.

ASSEMBLY

Serving this salad is just a matter of choosing a plate that will work with the variety of colors and textures. Here we used bright red to contrast the green of the leaves. Pile up the salad to get some height and look at the finished pile. Often there is one leaf that doesn't have the pretty side up and if you turn it over the whole salad looks more finished.

Grilled Quail in Soy Sauce
and Sake Marinade

Salad of Shrimp with
Chanterelles and Tomatoes

Focaccia with Mozzarella
and Anchovy Salad

Wild Rice with Pine Nuts and Sweet Peas

Sometimes it is wonderful to take a dish apart and put it back together in a whole new way. That's what we did with one of our favorite foods: a sandwich of sliced focaccia bread layered with arugula, anchovies, and fresh mozzarella cheese.

For our bento, we tossed those same ingredients into a salad of assorted shapes, colors, and lines—preserving the satisfying balance of flavors. We like to think of this as a deconstructed ham and cheese sandwich: It tastes just like one (even without the ham) and might be better than the original.

You can quickly toss together two more mixtures of complementary ingredients. Poached shrimp, sautéed chanterelle mushrooms, and plum tomato wedges provide a cooling and colorful element in the meal. Baby sweet peas and pine nuts add sweetness and depth to wild rice. And even though it stands alone on its dish, the grilled quail presents a surprising host of flavors, with salt, spice, and heat drawn from its Oriental marinade.

Every food can cook and then rest until cool and there is ample opportunity for creative presentation in plating each dish and then arranging your box. We were fortunate to have the deep blue fan-shaped bowl for the rice and to find that it fit so well within our "octagonal" shokado box, adding variety and a dynamic diagonal line to the design.

Though you may not have dishes or a frame in these unusual shapes, the menu itself offers a rich assortment of food colors and forms. Two food elements in particular can make strong visual statements: The grill marks on the pieces of quail may be set in an interesting direction. And the curve of the bright shrimp should also be arranged to catch the eye. Try standing the shrimp up to make a vertical arch within your composition.

Grilled Quail in Soy Sauce and Sake Marinade

Makes 4 bento servings

1 cup soy sauce

3 tablespoons fresh lime juice

2 tablespoons sake, Japanese rice wine, or dry sherry

1 tablespoon whole coriander seeds, cracked

1 teaspoon whole black peppercorns, coarsely cracked

½ teaspoon hot red pepper flakes

4 boneless quail (see Note)

1 tablespoon extra-virgin olive oil

2 tablespoons finely chopped fresh chives or scallions, for garnish

In a shallow nonreactive pan, combine the soy sauce, lime juice, sake, coriander seeds, cracked black peppercorns, and pepper flakes. Set the quail in the marinade and refrigerate for 2 to 3 hours, turning once. Do not marinate for more than 3 hours or the quail will absorb too much salt.

Prepare a grill or heat a sauté pan over high heat for 1 minute. Remove the quail from the marinade, dry them, then rub them with the olive oil. Grill or sauté the quail for 2 minutes on each side, or until the quail is browned and the skin looks crisp.

continued

Remove the quail to a cutting board and let it rest for 5 minutes. With a sharp knife, cut the legs off and separate the thigh from the drumstick. Separate the 2 breasts, leaving a wing attached to each half.

A S S E M B L Y

Serve 1 quail per person and arrange on a small plate. Put the legs on top of the breasts, showing off the nicest grill marks. Sprinkle chives over the quail.

N O T E   These quail come with drumsticks and wing bones intact and a wire V-pin to facilitate cooking and eating. They can be bought at many specialty butcher shops and supermarkets across the country or by mail order from D'Artagnan (1-800-327-8246).

Salad of Shrimp with Chanterelles and Tomatoes

Makes 4 bento servings

¼ cup kosher salt or 2 tablespoons iodized table salt

12 ounces shrimp, peeled and deveined (use size 25 to 30 to the pound, which are about 2 bites each)

8 ounces chanterelle mushrooms, wiped clean with a damp cloth

2 tablespoons extra-virgin olive oil

Salt and freshly ground black pepper

2 ripe plum tomatoes or substitute other ripe tomatoes

Fill a 1½-quart saucepan with 1 quart of water and the salt. This will be as salty as seawater. Add the shrimp and cook over high heat for 3 to 4 minutes, until just barely done. Remove to a plate and spread in a single layer to cool quickly to room temperature.

If the mushrooms are large, cut them into bite-size pieces. Heat the olive oil in a skillet over high heat. Season the mushrooms with salt and pepper, add to the skillet, and sauté until soft, about 5 minutes, taking care not to burn them. Remove the mushrooms to a plate and let cool.

Cut the tomatoes into wedges and season with salt and pepper.

In a bowl, toss the shrimp, mushrooms, tomatoes, and any juices from the cooling plates together and serve.

Focaccia with Mozzarella and Anchovy Salad

1 tin flat anchovy fillets, cut lengthwise into strips (save the oil the anchovies
   came packed in)

2 tablespoons extra-virgin olive oil

1 tablespoon balsamic vinegar

Freshly ground black pepper

2 cups loosely packed, washed, arugula leaves

1 small focaccia bread (see Note)

4 ounces fresh mozzarella cheese, preferably bocconcini (see Note), cut into
   bite-size pieces

In a medium bowl, mix together 1 tablespoon of oil from the anchovies with the olive oil. Whisk in the vinegar and season to taste with pepper.

Toss the arugula leaves in the vinaigrette to coat each leaf lightly and place in bowls. Scatter the bread, anchovies, and cheese on the leaves. Often there is one spinach leaf that doesn't have the pretty side up and if you turn it over the whole salad looks more finished.

NOTE   Focaccia is a rich, flat, Italian bread. If it is not available, substitute any chewy French or Italian bread.

If bocconcini are not available, use larger fresh mozzarella and cut into ¼-inch slices.

Wild Rice with Pine Nuts and Sweet Peas

1 cup wild rice

3 cups chicken stock

Kosher salt and freshly ground black pepper, to taste

½ cup fresh or frozen baby sweet peas

¼ cup pine nuts (pignolis), lightly toasted (see Note)

Bring the wild rice, chicken stock, and salt and pepper to a boil in a 6-cup saucepan over high heat. Reduce the heat to low and simmer, covered, for 45 minutes, or until half the grains have split open. Transfer the rice to a bowl and let cool to room temperature, stirring occasionally.

Bring a pot of lightly salted water to a boil over high heat and add the peas to blanch for 15 seconds, or until they turn bright green. Drain the peas, refresh in iced, salted water, and set aside.

Stir the peas and pine nuts into the cooked wild rice and correct the seasoning.

ASSEMBLY

We chose an unusual plate shape for this dish. The pale pine nuts stand out vividly against the dark rice on the dark plate. Make sure the peas and pine nuts are visible when you mound the rice on the plate.

NOTE   Toast the pine nuts in a single layer in a 325°F oven for 7 minutes, or until golden brown.

Summer

Chicken Breast with Corn, Walnuts, and Cilantro

Tomato and Bread Salad

Seared Tuna with Sesame Seed Crust and Caramel Soy

Japanese Rice with Bacon and Sun-dried Tomato

The big, bold shapes in this summery bento may catch the eye first—the perfect sphere of bacon-and-tomato-flavored rice and the luminous, almost translucent squares of seared tuna. Yet it is the simple pile of *panzanella*, the fresh bread and tomato salad in the front left compartment, that best exemplifies the subtleties of bento design.

How do you make a pile of food look good? Every cook who loves presentation faces this challenge frequently. We have some principles on the subject. First, prepare the food carefully: Beautifully cooked food will look beautiful even in a plain pile. And make the mound with consciousness—and confidence. At The Quilted Giraffe the phrase was "Make it look like a Zen monk tossed it on the plate."

Still, the lovely dish of *panzanella* is not only a spiritual construction. Here, we built the mound carefully in two steps, first creating a base and then adding another portion to give it height. We deliberately left space around the food—utilizing the plate pattern as a design element, creating shadows, and lending more height and prominence to the pile.

This dish stands out also for its complex visual texture. There was a time when, as avowed modernists, we used only large white plates for presentation. We still like stark, minimalist backgrounds for densely textured or multicolored food, as the chicken and corn salad is presented in a plain, solid color bowl. But we took a different tack with the *panzanella*, purposely plating this "busy" dish on a "busy" plate. By itself, it looks lush and fancy, and creates dynamic contrast with the other elements of the bento.

There's nothing theoretical about the food here: This meal is a perfect refreshment from the heat of a summer day. Tomatoes, herbs, olive oil, and balsamic vinegar infuse the chunks of sourdough bread with sweetness. Chicken briefly poached, then cooled in stock and vermouth remains creamy, matched against the crunch of walnuts, sweet corn just off the cob, and the zing of cilantro.

The rich, pure taste of the just-seared tuna is spectacular. It is complemented by the salty sweetness of the caramel soy dipping sauce and the toasty crunch of its black and white sesame seed crust. The tuna (as all the dishes in this meal) can be prepared well ahead of serving, though it should be sliced at the last minute to preserve its moistness. The sphere of brightly flavored rice is easy and fun to make, simply rolled in your hands.

Chicken Breast with Corn, Walnuts, and Cilantro

Makes 4 bento servings

2 cups chicken stock, seasoned with salt and pepper

4 ounces (½ cup) white vermouth (preferably Noilly Prat brand; see Note)

2 large skinless, boneless chicken breast halves, about 5 ounces each

2 ears of corn

6 fresh cilantro sprigs

¼ cup walnut halves

2 tablespoons olive oil

Salt and freshly ground black pepper

About 1½ to 2 hours in advance, heat the stock and vermouth in a large skillet over medium-high heat. When the stock is simmering, add the chicken to poach. Reduce the heat as necessary and do not allow the liquid to boil, just simmer until the chicken is firm on one side, then turn and poach on the other side. Turn off the heat and let the breasts cool in the stock.

Bring a large pot of boiling, salted water to a boil and add the ears of corn. Cook for 1 minute. Drain the corn and cut the kernels off the cob.

Wash the cilantro and pick the leaves off the stems.

Cut the cooled chicken breasts into 1-inch cubes and toss in a bowl with the corn, cilantro, walnuts, olive oil, and salt and pepper to taste.

N O T E A medium-bodied, full-flavored dry white wine may be substituted for the vermouth if necessary. The flavor of the recipe will be somewhat different than we intended.

Summer

Japanese Rice with Bacon and Sun-dried Tomato

Makes 4 bento servings

1 cup short-grain Japanese rice

6 pieces of sun-dried tomato, rehydrated for 15 minutes in warm water

4 strips of bacon, cooked crisp and crumbled

Salt and freshly ground black pepper

Lightly rinse the rice. Put the rice in a small pot with 1 cup of water and let it soak for 30 minutes. Stir the rice well and place over high heat. Let the rice come to a boil and then stir well again. Reduce the heat to the lowest setting possible, cover the pot with a tight-fitting lid, and let simmer for 11 minutes. Then move the rice off the heat and let sit, still covered, for 5 minutes more.

Chop the rehydrated tomato into pea-sized pieces.

Transfer the rice to a bowl, stir well, and let cool for 10 minutes. Stir in the bacon and tomato and season to taste with salt and pepper. Use wet hands to roll the rice into perfect spheres.

Seared Tuna with Sesame Seed Crust and Caramel Soy

Makes 4 bento servings

½ cup sugar

1 tablespoon water

½ cup soy sauce

2 cloves garlic, sliced

3 slices of ginger (the size of a quarter)

¾ pound sushi-quality tuna, cut from the center part of the loin

6 tablespoons sesame seeds, both black and white if you can get them

¼ cup peanut oil

Salt

In a very small saucepan, bring the sugar and water to a boil over high heat, stirring occasionally. When the mixture starts to turn brown around the edges, remove it from the heat and let it turn to a dark honey color. Note that once the sugar starts to caramelize it is very hot and will caramelize rapidly. Stand back and carefully pour in the soy sauce. The caramel will generate a lot of steam and may spatter, so hold your hand out of the way. Stir in the garlic and ginger as the caramel is cooling. Let them infuse at room temperature for at least 30 minutes. Strain out the ginger and garlic before serving.

Wet the tuna with fresh cool water and roll in sesame seeds so that each surface is evenly coated. Heat the peanut oil in a skillet over medium-high heat. Season the fish lightly with salt, place in the skillet, and sear for about 1 minute or less on each side. The seeds should be toasted and light brown. The inside of the tuna should be quite rare. The heat should not be too high or the seeds will burn.

Let the tuna cool and then slice it thinly with a very sharp knife. Serve with the caramel soy as a dipping sauce.

Tomato and Bread Salad

2 slices stale sourdough bread, torn into ½-inch pieces, about 2 cups

2 ripe plum tomatoes, roughly chopped

1 tablespoon chopped fresh flat-leaf parsley

1 tablespoon fresh thyme leaves

1 teaspoon chopped fresh oregano

1 tablespoon balsamic vinegar

2 tablespoons extra-virgin olive oil

Salt and freshly ground black pepper

Soak the bread in a bowl of water for 15 minutes, then drain and squeeze the bread dry. Tear it into small pieces.

In a bowl, mix the bread with the tomatoes, herbs, vinegar, and olive oil, season to taste with salt and pepper, and let the salad sit for 2 hours.

Stir the salad once more, adjust the seasoning, and serve at room temperature.

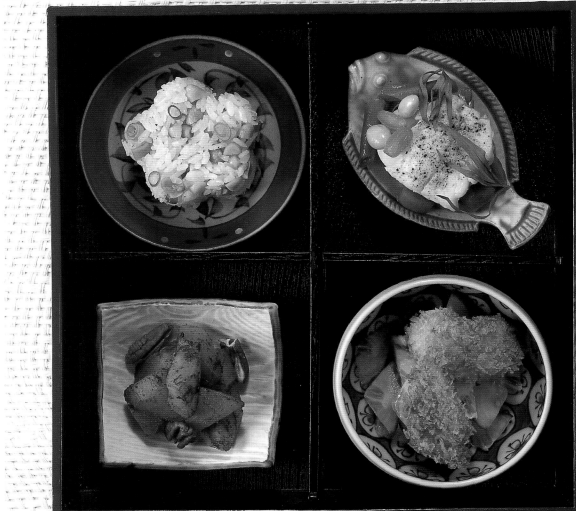

Chicken Nuggets with Spicy Cucumber

Curried Acorn Squash with Pecans

Japanese Rice with Salted Peanuts and Scallions

Braised Cod with Green Beans, Cranberry Beans, and Flat Beans

A food as universally loved as fried chicken must have a place in a bento menu. Here it is a surprisingly easy, and elegant, component of a tasty, many-textured summer meal.

Much of the sensual pleasure of fried food—the stimulation of both eye and mouth—comes from a perfectly colored, crisp exterior. We were delighted to discover that we got both by using *panko*, dried Japanese bread crumbs, as a crust. The unusual, elongated shape of the crumbs and their high sugar content (from honey in the bread) creates a surface with tempting depth, golden color, and visual texture—and the crunch is as fabulous as it looks. Although you may use ordinary dried white bread crumbs as a substitute, we urge you to find *panko* at an Asian food market (and we give you some mail-order sources on page 152).

Careful deep-frying is a must: Use oil at the proper temperature and blot the chicken pieces on absorbent paper immediately as they are taken from the frying pot. Care will be rewarded with a deep color, satisfying crunch, and a virtually greaseless morsel of chicken.

A simple, almost instant cucumber pickle provides an elegant, shimmering bed for the chicken as well as a terrific taste contrast. Tossed with champagne vinegar and a touch of Vietnamese chili paste, the thin triangular slices are at once cool and piquant, wet and crunchy.

The other dishes also display simple techniques that create flavor, texture, and visual appeal all at once. Small angular chunks of acorn squash are sautéed with mild curry powder and then briefly steamed. This quick double cooking yields a lovely sweetness and flecks of brown on the golden squash, a color echoed by the pecan garnish. Crushed salted peanuts and rounds of sliced scallion likewise lend a pleasant saltiness, textural variety, and a colorful, variegated surface to the blossom-shaped rice.

One of our favorite visual accents comes from the paper-thin slivers of Romano bean that dot the surface of the braised cod. We enjoy taking an everyday food—a string bean—

and giving it a new shape that removes it from normal reference, in this case simply by cutting across its usual axis. The flavors of the beans and the fish meld when they are poached together in water and vermouth, and the dish, infused with tarragon, is a moist and succulent foil to the rest of the meal.

Chicken Nuggets with Spicy Cucumber

Makes 4 bento servings

1 quart peanut or canola oil

1 seedless cucumber

¼ teaspoon Vietnamese chili paste (or Tabasco or other hot sauce)

3 tablespoons champagne or white wine vinegar

Salt and freshly ground black pepper

1 pound skinless, boneless chicken breast or thigh

Flour

1 beaten egg

1 cup dried bread crumbs, preferably *panko* (a Japanese variety)

Heat the oil to 350°F in a heavy 2-quart saucepan.

Cut the cucumber in quarters lengthwise, then cut into ¼-inch slices on an angle. In a bowl, toss the cucumber slices with the chili paste, vinegar, and salt and pepper to taste and set aside.

Cut the chicken into 1-inch cubes and season with salt and pepper. Dredge the chicken cubes in the flour, dip them in the beaten egg, and roll in the bread crumbs to coat evenly. Fry the chicken pieces in 2 batches in the hot oil for approximately 3 minutes for breast meat or 5 minutes for thigh meat, until the crust is golden brown. Lift the chicken from the oil and drain immediately on paper towels.

ASSEMBLY

We chose a deep plate that contrasts with the texture of the pickles. Mound the cucumber slices tightly in the center of the plate and prop the chicken nuggets up against them.

Summer

Curried Acorn Squash with Pecans

Makes 4 bento servings

1 medium acorn squash

1 tablespoon sweet butter

1½ teaspoons mild curry powder

¼ cup water

Salt and freshly ground black pepper

½ cup lightly toasted pecans (see Note)

Peel the acorn squash and cut it into 1-inch strips, then into 1-inch chunks on an angle.

In a skillet, heat the butter over medium heat. Add the curry powder and stir for 1 minute.

Add the acorn squash, water, and salt and pepper to taste, then stir thoroughly. Let the squash cook, covered, over low heat until the water has evaporated and the squash is tender, about 10 minutes. Taste and adjust the seasoning.

ASSEMBLY

We chose a beige and brown shallow plate that echoes the colors of this dish. Stack the squash pieces in the center with as many angles showing as possible. Scatter the pecan pieces over the squash with the pretty side up.

NOTE Toast the pecans in a single layer in a 325°F oven until golden brown, about 7 minutes.

Japanese Rice with Salted Peanuts and Scallions

Makes 4 bento servings

2 cups short-grain Japanese rice

5 tablespoons salted peanuts

2 scallions, sliced thinly across

1 teaspoon peanut oil

Kosher salt and freshly ground black pepper

Lightly rinse the rice in a sieve until all the rice is wet. Put it in a 6-cup saucepan with 2 cups water and let it soak for 30 minutes.

Crush the peanuts lightly to the size of whole peppercorns. This is easy to do by pressing a small, heavy saucepan on the peanuts with a rocking motion.

Stir the rice well and place the saucepan over high heat. Let the rice come to a boil. Stir it again and turn the heat down as low as possible. Cover the saucepan with a tight-fitting lid and let simmer for 11 minutes. Move the rice off the heat and let it sit, covered, for 5 minutes.

Transfer the rice to a bowl, stir well, and let cool for 10 minutes. Fold in the peanuts, scallions, oil, and season with salt and pepper to taste. Shape the rice in a mold (see page 20).

ASSEMBLY

Choose a simple, colorful plate that contrasts in both shape and color with the rice. For instance, the complex floral shape here is on a simple circle and the bright red rim of the plate sets off the calm colors of the rice.

Braised Cod with Green Beans, Cranberry Beans, and Flat Beans

Makes 4 bento servings

8 ounces codfish fillet

4 ounces total of a mixture of green string beans, fresh cranberry beans, and green
   Romano beans (see Note)

3 or 4 fresh tarragon sprigs

3 tablespoons extra-virgin olive oil

½ cup water

½ cup vermouth

Salt and freshly ground black pepper

Cut the cod into 4 evenly sized pieces.

Trim the stems off the green beans and cut into 1-inch slices on the diagonal. Shell the cranberry beans and cut the Romano beans into ¼-inch slices across the beans.

Pull the tarragon leaves off the stems and set the leaves aside in the refrigerator for garnish. Put the stems into a shallow saucepan.

Add the olive oil, water, and vermouth to the saucepan with the tarragon stems. Add all the beans, bring to a boil over high heat, and cook, covered, for 5 minutes.

Season the fish pieces with salt and pepper and place in the saucepan on top of the beans. Cover the pot and cook over medium heat until the fish is cooked and the beans are tender, about 4 minutes more. Remove the tarragon stems.

To serve, arrange some of the cooked beans on each plate and place a piece of fish on top of them. Garnish with the reserved tarragon leaves.

N O T E   If fresh cranberry beans or green Romano beans are unavailable, use any combination of fresh pale beans offering color and flavor contrasts.

*S*callops and Mussels with Corn,
Orzo, and Tomato

*S*weet and Snow Pea Soup

*J*apanese Rice with Black Olives
and Orange Zest

*G*rilled Steak with Red Onions

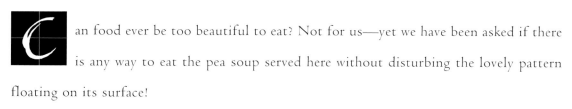an food ever be too beautiful to eat? Not for us—yet we have been asked if there is any way to eat the pea soup served here without disturbing the lovely pattern floating on its surface!

While you might choose just to look at this bento—with its striking colors and dramatic composition—we hope you will cook it, eat it, and enjoy its celebration of summertime tastes: fresh peas, tomatoes, corn, and grilled steak. These dishes are as delicious to eat as they are beautiful to look at.

There is much natural sweetness and simplicity here. Snow peas and sweet peas are cooked briefly in chicken stock, then puréed to make the brilliantly colored soup. (The crème fraîche garnish is so easy you won't mind messing it up.) Next to it, a sauté of corn, diced ripe tomatoes, sweet basil, and cooked orzo pasta are matched with the briny sweetness of seared scallops and steamed mussels.

The day before this meal is prepared, the steak is marinated in sake, soy sauce, and coriander seeds; the accompanying onions in a cumin-flavored vinegar. After this long infusion, the quick, hot grilling brings up new layers of sweetness, spice, and saltiness. And finally, the maple leaf–shaped rice brings bright and piquant notes of orange zest and black olives.

We are excited here by the interplay of vibrant colors in both the food and serving vessels. For many years, we have plated food on purple dishes—and in related shades of mauve and violet—with great effect. Here, the verdant soup in the purple bowl is electrifying. And the cool white and blue tones of the rice leaf and bowl are a dramatic contrast to the intensely red meat and onions. White or blue dishes, though most common, are not the only choices for the bento cook: Don't be afraid to explore a more daring palette of color.

A note on shaping the maple leaf rice: We used a rice mold, but you can use any of the other rice-shaping techniques in this book.

Scallops and Mussels with Corn, Orzo, and Tomato

Makes 4 bento servings

½ cup orzo (a dried rice-shaped pasta)

¼ cup olive oil

1 scallion, finely sliced

2 ears corn, kernels cut off the cob

1 red bell pepper, seeded and diced

1 large ripe tomato, diced

1 tablespoon sweet butter

2 tablespoons white vermouth

2 heaping tablespoons fresh basil, cut into thin strips

Salt and freshly ground black pepper

4 large scallops or 12 small scallops, cleaned and dried

4 mussels, bearded and washed

Bring a large pot of salted water to a boil. Add the orzo and cook until al dente, 10 to 12 minutes. Drain and set aside.

Heat 2 tablespoons of the olive oil in a sauté pan over medium heat. Add the scallion, corn, red pepper, tomato, cooked orzo, butter, and vermouth. Cook for 2 minutes at a low boil to just melt the butter, warm through the vegetables, and bring the sauce together. Do not overcook or the sauce will separate. Stir in the basil and season with salt and pepper. Set aside and keep warm.

continued

Heat a sauté pan over high heat. Add the remaining 2 tablespoons olive oil and sear the scallops for 1 minute on one side, then turn over and let cook 1 minute more. When the scallops are cooked, remove from the pan. Add the mussels to the hot pan with ¼ cup water and cover. Let the mussels steam just until open, 1 to 2 minutes. Remove the mussels from the pan. Continue to cook the liquid in the pan until it is reduced by half, 1 or 2 minutes, and pour into the vegetable and orzo mix. Serve the shellfish on top of the vegetable mix.

Sweet and Snow Pea Soup

Makes 4 bento servings

1 cup water

1 cup chicken stock

4½ cups tightly packed snow peas

2 cups shelled fresh peas or frozen baby peas

2 tablespoons heavy cream

Salt and freshly ground black pepper

2 tablespoons crème fraîche or sour cream (see Note)

5 chives, cut into ½-inch lengths

In a pot over high heat, bring the water and stock to a boil. Add the snow peas to the pot, reduce the heat to low, and simmer until tender, about 5 minutes. Add the sweet peas and cream. Let simmer for 1 minute, then pour the soup into a blender. Blend the soup on high speed until smooth, about 3 minutes. Pass the soup through a fine strainer and season to taste. Garnish with crème fraîche and chives.

NOTE   Crème fraîche is a cultured cream product that is slightly sour in taste. It is available in gourmet shops and some supermarkets.

Japanese Rice with Black Olives and Orange Zest

Makes 4 bento servings

2 cups short-grain Japanese rice

⅓ cup kalamata or other good-quality black olives

1 tablespoon extra-virgin olive oil

Zest of 1 orange

1 teaspoon salt

Freshly ground black pepper

Lightly rinse the rice. Put the rice in a small pot with 2 cups of water and let it soak for 30 minutes.

Pit the black olives and cut into small pieces.

Stir the rice well and place over high heat. Let it come to a boil, then stir well again and turn the heat down to the lowest possible setting. Cover the pot with a tight-fitting lid and let simmer for 11 minutes. Remove from the heat and let sit, still covered, for 5 minutes more.

Transfer the rice to a bowl, stir well, and let cool for 10 minutes. Stir in the chopped olives, olive oil, and orange zest. Season with salt and pepper to taste.

Press the rice in a rice mold or shape by hand, and serve. Japanese rice is very sticky. To keep the rice from sticking to the rice mold, keep both pieces of the mold in water. Fill the mold ⅔ full with rice and press down with the top part firmly enough for the rice to stick together, but not so firmly that the rice gets mashed. Release the rice from the mold and put on a plate.

Grilled Steak with Red Onions

Makes 4 bento servings

1 cup soy sauce

2 tablespoons fresh lime juice

¼ cup sake, Japanese rice wine, or dry sherry

1 tablespoon cracked coriander seeds

1 teaspoon coarsely cracked black peppercorns

1 pound sirloin steak

2 medium red onions

1 tablespoon ground cumin

1 tablespoon red wine vinegar

1 tablespoon extra-virgin olive oil

1 teaspoon salt

Freshly ground black pepper

In a large bowl, mix together the soy sauce, lime juice, sake, coriander seeds, and peppercorns and let the steak marinate in this mixture, covered, for 12 to 36 hours in the refrigerator.

Peel the red onions, leaving the root ends intact. This will hold the onion layers together during grilling. Cut the onions into eighths through the root.

In a bowl, mix together the cumin, vinegar, olive oil, salt, and pepper to taste. Add the onion pieces and toss gently to coat. Marinate, covered, overnight in the refrigerator or up to 2 hours at room temperature.

continued

Let the steak come to room temperature. Preheat a barbecue or stove-top grill. Season the steak with salt and pepper to taste and then grill it 4 or 5 minutes on each side, leaving it rare. Let the steak rest for 10 minutes.

Meanwhile, grill the onions until they are soft, about 5 minutes. Taste for seasoning. Correct as necessary. Slice the steak thinly with a sharp knife and serve with the onions.

Fall

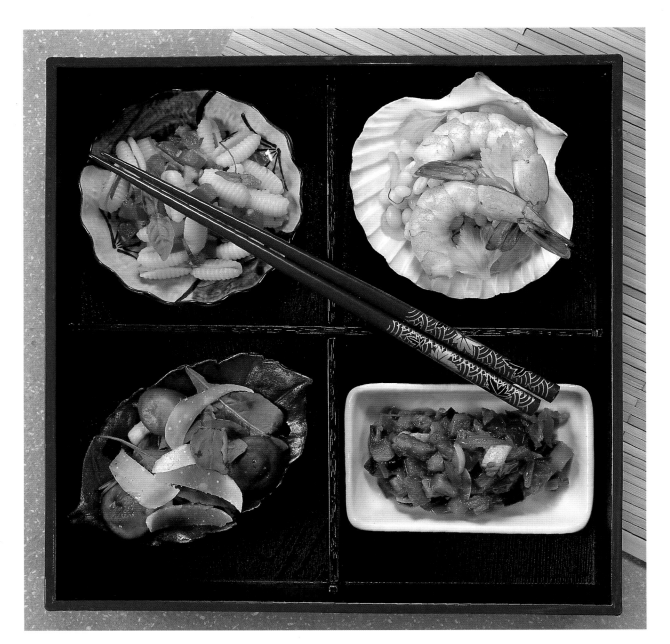

Arugula Salad with Parmesan and Pickled Shiitake Mushrooms

Ratatouille

Pasta with Raw Tomato Sauce

Poached Shrimp with White Beans, Celery, and Saffron

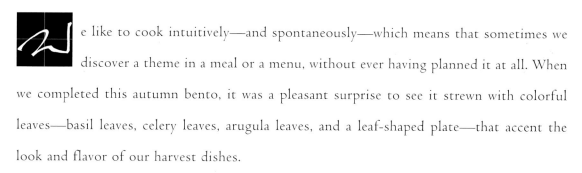

We like to cook intuitively—and spontaneously—which means that sometimes we discover a theme in a meal or a menu, without ever having planned it at all. When we completed this autumn bento, it was a pleasant surprise to see it strewn with colorful leaves—basil leaves, celery leaves, arugula leaves, and a leaf-shaped plate—that accent the look and flavor of our harvest dishes.

We did plan a meal with Mediterranean flavor and drew on three simple preparations from our days at La Colombe d'Or in New York (a famed showcase for the foods of Provence). Large shrimp are served on a bed of white beans and celery. Small pasta are tossed with a sauce of raw plum tomatoes and basil. And ratatouille brings together the sweetest vegetables and herbs from the late season garden: eggplant, sweet bell pepper, tomatoes, zucchini and summer squash, and basil and thyme. As a delicious contrast in the fourth dish, lightly pickled shiitake mushrooms, in a salad of arugula, lends a touch of Asia with slivers of Parmesan cheese bringing it back to the Mediterranean.

There is another flavor theme winding through this bento: the subtle use of acidic elements—four different vinegars and lemon juice—in each of the preparations. The shiitake mushrooms, simmered and cooled with white wine vinegar and low-acid rice vinegar, are a bright, perfect match for the Parmesan—yet without the sharpness of conventional mushrooms à la grecque. A different and even milder acidic note comes from the touch of champagne vinegar with which the white beans are seasoned. In the two other dishes, the acidic element is almost hidden but important: Balsamic vinegar (a very low-acid condiment) intensifies the sweetness of the raw tomatoes on the pasta, and lemon juice serves to brighten all the other flavors in the ratatouille.

Interested cooks should note another culinary technique employed here: A small amount of mushroom cooking liquid is used to dress the arugula leaves, and the shrimp poaching liquid is similarly used to dress the white beans. These cooking essences can carry the flavor through to integrate the whole dish.

A word on design: This is a composition of delicate, bite-size food (with the exception of the large shrimp and Parmesan curls) and each dish must be carefully presented. The vegetables in the ratatouille and the tomatoes in the pasta should be finely and uniformly diced; the pasta should be small and delicate; and each shiitake mushroom should be whole and perfect, a jewel in the salad.

Arugula Salad with Parmesan and Pickled Shiitake Mushrooms

Makes 4 bento servings

2 tablespoons rice vinegar

2 tablespoons white wine vinegar

2 tablespoons sugar

1 tablespoon salt

1½ tablespoons water

2 ounces fresh shiitake mushrooms, wiped with a damp cloth

3 tablespoons extra-virgin olive oil

1-ounce block Parmesan cheese, for shaving

2 cups loosely packed washed arugula leaves

To pickle the shiitake mushrooms, combine the first 5 ingredients in a pot and bring to a simmer over medium-high heat to dissolve the sugar and salt. Add the shiitake mushrooms, turn off the heat, and let cool in the liquid.

Make a vinaigrette using 1 tablespoon of the cooled mushroom liquid, whisking in the olive oil. Use a vegetable peeler to shave the Parmesan cheese to get long, thin curls.

ASSEMBLY

Toss the arugula with the vinaigrette and arrange on plates. Place the mushrooms and Parmesan curls on top.

Ratatouille

Makes 4 bento servings and more

3 tablespoons extra-virgin olive oil

1 small onion, diced

3 cloves garlic, crushed and minced

1 bay leaf

1 small Italian eggplant, about ½ pound, cut into ½-inch dice

1 sweet red bell pepper, seeded and diced

4 plum tomatoes, diced but not peeled or seeded

Salt

1 small zucchini, about ¼ pound, cut into ½-inch dice

1 small yellow summer squash, about ¼ pound, cut into ½-inch dice

1 tablespoon chopped fresh thyme

2 tablespoons chopped fresh basil

Freshly ground black pepper

Fresh lemon juice

In a 2-quart saucepan over low heat, add the olive oil, onion, garlic, and bay leaf and cook gently for 5 minutes. Add the eggplant, red pepper, tomatoes with all their juices, and a large pinch of salt. Cover and cook for 10 minutes more. If the mixture seems dry at this point, add ½ cup of water.

Add the squashes and thyme and cook, covered, for 30 minutes more. Stir in the basil and correct the seasoning with more salt, if necessary, pepper, and a few drops of lemon juice. The lemon juice will brighten the flavor.

continued

Simple Menus for the Bento Box

Serve at room temperature. Ratatouille should not be served refrigerator cold.

This recipe will make more than what is required for 4 people in this bento. However, it will keep for several days in the refrigerator, tightly covered, to be used at another time.

Pasta with Raw Tomato Sauce

Makes 4 bento servings

½ shallot, chopped

1 clove garlic, minced

2 ripe plum tomatoes, cut into small dice but not peeled or seeded

3 branches fresh basil, large leaves cut into thin strips and baby leaves saved for garnish

1 teaspoon balsamic vinegar

¼ cup extra-virgin olive oil

Salt and freshly ground black pepper

1 cup small dried macaroni

Place the first 6 ingredients in a porcelain or stainless steel bowl. Season to taste with salt and pepper and mix very well. Let sit at room temperature at least 1 hour. Correct the seasoning if necessary.

Cook the macaroni in a pot of at least 2 quarts of boiling, salted water until al dente, 8 to 10 minutes. Drain and toss the hot macaroni with the raw tomato sauce.

Serve at room temperature.

Poached Shrimp with White Beans, Celery, and Saffron

Makes 4 bento servings

½ cup dry white beans (cannellini beans or French navy beans are delicious)

1 tablespoon champagne vinegar or good-quality white wine vinegar

Salt and freshly ground black pepper

1 tablespoon extra-virgin olive oil

8 large shrimp

3 stalks celery and some of the light green leaves from the center

⅛ teaspoon saffron threads

Soak the beans overnight in a large bowl with enough cold water to cover by 2 inches.

Drain the beans and place them in a 2-quart pot with 1 quart of fresh water. Bring to a boil over high heat, then reduce the heat to medium and simmer until the beans are soft, about 40 minutes. (One method of checking the beans is to blow on a few; if the skin splits, they are done.)

Drain the beans and while still hot toss them in a large bowl with the vinegar. Season with salt and pepper and then toss with the olive oil. Let the beans cool.

In a small shallow pan, place the shrimp in 2 inches of cold water that has been salted to the salinity of sea water. Turn the heat to high. Stir slowly and when the shrimp have turned pink and feel firm, remove them from the water, spread in a single layer on a plate, and let cool to room temperature. The shrimp will never be tough when cooked in this manner.

continued

Wash the celery stalks and slice them into very thin slices. Toss the celery with the cooled beans, 2 or 3 tablespoons of the shrimp poaching liquid, and the saffron threads. Wayne loves the intense color contrast of the saffron threads against the white beans and green celery.

A S S E M B L Y

To serve, place the poached shrimp on the beans and garnish with the reserved celery leaves.

Butternut Squash Soup with Parmesan

Japanese Rice with Chicken
and Soy Glaze

Tempura Soft-Shell Crabs
on Spicy Watercress

Asparagus with Portobello Mushrooms

This is an autumnal menu of great textures and flavors from the ocean and the woods. Cooks will also find in this meal several simple yet pleasing techniques that serve well on many other occasions.

The year's last soft-shell crabs appear by late September or early October and we have included them in this menu as a last hurrah. In late April and early May, the first ones of the season begin to appear from the southern Eastern Shore around South Carolina, and they progress northward as the weather gets warmer. The season's last yield is from the Jersey Shore, and these are what we will have here. Try to get the smallest crabs you can, as they are the sweetest and most tender. Resist the temptation to buy frozen ones because they are probably from last year's harvest and will be watery and not very flavorful when they defrost.

Perfectly fried soft-shell crab demand care and attention—for just a few minutes. Our tempura batter, properly made to the consistency of cream, provides a tasty, crisp casing for the crabs. Too-thick batters or breadings—or too cool or overheated oil—will ruin this delicacy. With oil exactly at 350°F, you will quickly create a thin layer of crunch and a creamy interior. In this bento, the crab's sweetness is piqued with the spicy and acidic notes (and colorful accents) of watercress and roasted tomato.

We love the portobello mushrooms bathed in olive oil and roasted in a slow oven, an unusual preparation that intensifies the deep woodsy flavor and adds to its succulent meatiness. More flavorful than grilled or sautéed mushrooms, they are an especially good pairing with crisp asparagus. We hope you will enjoy these mushroom caps many times. Try them as a sandwich on a loaf of *ciabbata* or other crusty hearth bread with a spicy mayonnaise and some roasted tomatoes.

The simple flower shape of Japanese rice in the corner is in fact bursting with flavors. After it is cooked and cooled, the rice is mixed with bits of cooked chicken and seasoned with soy sauce, dry mustard, and sugar. This instantly transformed rice—enlivened with salt, sweet, heat, and spice—is a method you will want to use many times.

Another textural touch to be remembered by the clever chef comes from the curls of Parmesan that float on the surface of the soup. More garnish than seasoning, they lend crunch, saltiness, and lovely curving lines—far more interesting than grated cheese or common croutons!

Speaking of lines and design, the oyster shell, with its reference to the sea, makes an appropriate vessel for the crab and also creates a graceful curve in the box. The asparagus forms another axis to lead the eye. We noted with particular pleasure how the golden circle of soup captures our attention first, just as golden quinoa does in another bento. With brilliant orange color and rich flavor, unclouded by milk or cream, it is the radiant heart of the box, as well as a tempting start to the meal.

Butternut Squash Soup with Parmesan

Makes 4 bento servings

½ small onion, finely diced (about ¼ cup)

1 tablespoon sweet butter

1 medium butternut squash, peeled and cut into ½-inch chunks (about 2 cups)

2 cups chicken stock

Salt and freshly ground black pepper

1-ounce block Parmesan cheese, for shaving

In a large saucepan over low heat, gently cook the onion in the butter until soft and transparent but not colored, about 7 minutes.

Add the squash, stock, and salt and pepper to taste and simmer, covered, until the squash is soft, 15 to 25 minutes.

While the soup is cooking, use a vegetable peeler to cut long curled shavings from the chunk of Parmesan cheese.

When the squash is soft, blend the soup until it is very smooth. Adjust the seasoning and serve with Parmesan cheese curls on top.

Japanese Rice with Chicken and Soy Glaze

Makes 4 bento servings

1 tablespoon soy sauce

1 tablespoon dry mustard powder

1 tablespoon sugar

2 cups short-grain Japanese rice

½ cup cooked chicken meat

Kosher salt

Freshly ground black pepper

In a small bowl, mix the soy sauce, mustard powder, and sugar together. Cover tightly and let sit overnight.

Rinse the rice lightly. Put the rice in a small pot with 2 cups of water and let it soak for 30 minutes.

Chop the chicken in a food processor or with a knife until it is the size of whole peppercorns.

Stir the rice well and place over high heat. Let the rice come to a boil, stir it well again, and turn the heat down to the lowest setting possible. Cover the pot with a tight-fitting lid and let simmer for 11 minutes. Then move the rice off the heat and let it sit, still covered, for 5 minutes more.

Transfer the rice to a bowl, stir well, and let cool for 10 minutes. Stir in the chopped chicken and soy sauce mixture. Season with salt and pepper to taste.

Press the rice in a rice press or shape by hand and serve (see page 79).

Tempura Soft-Shell Crabs
on Spicy Watercress

Makes 4 bento servings

½ cup all-purpose flour

1 tablespoon cornstarch

½ teaspoon salt

¼ teaspoon baking powder

20 ounces club soda

2 teaspoons butter, melted

2 quarts peanut or canola oil

4 soft-shell crabs, fully cleaned and prepared for cooking

½ bunch watercress, washed and dried

4 to 8 slices roasted tomato (see Note)

To make the batter, sift all the dry ingredients together. Stir in the club soda and melted butter and let the batter rest for 30 minutes.

Preheat the oil in a 2-quart or larger pot over high heat to 350°F. (You will need a thermometer for best results.)

When ready to serve, dip the crabs into the tempura batter to coat and fry in hot oil over a medium flame for 2 to 3 minutes. (Reduce or increase the heat as necessary to maintain 350°F.) Cook 2 crabs at a time and drain on paper towels.

continued

Cut the crabs into quarters and serve them on the watercress with 1 or 2 pieces of roasted tomato slices.

NOTE   To roast tomatoes, preheat the oven to 350°F. Spread olive oil lightly on a baking tray, then salt and pepper the tray. Slice plum tomatoes in half lengthwise or good beefsteak tomatoes into ½-inch slices. Place the tomatoes on the prepared baking tray and season with salt and pepper, olive oil, chopped thyme, and garlic. Place the tray in the oven, turn the oven off, and keep closed overnight. The tomatoes will have shrunk to about half their original size.

Asparagus with Portobello Mushroooms

2 large portobello mushrooms, wiped clean with a damp cloth, stems separated from
   the caps
Salt and freshly ground black pepper
2 cups extra-virgin olive oil
1 small bunch asparagus, trimmed, washed, and cut into 2-inch lengths

Preheat the oven to 325°F.

Season the mushroom caps and stems with salt and pepper, place in a glass baking dish, and cover them with olive oil. Cover and roast the mushrooms in the oven until soft, about 45 minutes.

Let the mushrooms come to room temperature in the oil, then drain and cut into ¼-inch slices across the caps.

Bring a pot of salted water to a boil. Add the asparagus and blanch until barely tender, then stop the cooking by refreshing the asparagus in iced and salted water.

Drain the asparagus and serve with the mushroom slices on top. Use the reserved mushroom-flavored olive oil in salad dressings or as a condiment for steamed vegetables in another meal.

Curried Basmati Rice with Raisins

Salt-Cured Salmon with Fennel Salad

Braised Leeks with Pecorino Cheese

Rack of Lamb with Sweet Mustard Glaze

An elegant presentation, the curve of a lamb bone dramatically sweeping out of the frame, declares this bento to be a special occasion dinner. The home-cured salmon and flash-roasted rack of New Zealand lamb are rare treats (in two senses of the term). Both have a richness of flavor and sensual texture that belie their astonishing ease of preparation.

The salt cure for the salmon, which you will learn here (and nowhere else!), is a marvelous method of transforming raw fish into a succulent delicacy. It rivals fine gravlax and smoked salmons, like Nova—at a fraction of the expense and effort. You will bury a salmon fillet in kosher salt with aromatic spices. Six hours later it will be cured and ready to serve, sublimely perfumed with coriander and chives, sliced thinly, and arranged over a pile of lightly dressed fennel slivers, as we do in this bento.

The small New Zealand racks of lamb (now widely available in the United States) yield delicate portions of meat that fit wonderfully into a bento box—both in physical and aesthetic terms. It is important that the rack be well trimmed by your butcher: "Frenched to the eye," as we say, with its insulating cap of fat completely removed. For the bento, it is coated with a simple mix of Dijon mustard and sugar and roasted for just 10 minutes. The intense richness of the small chop is cut by the sweet and spicy glaze.

Accompanying these extravagant dishes are two distinctive preparations. Sweet leeks, braised in chicken stock and butter, enjoy an unusual and salty accent from sheep's milk pecorino cheese. Curried rice is a natural and traditional companion for lamb. We add several layers of flavor, from the nutty quality of aromatic basmati rice and from raisins plumped in Earl Grey tea, which passes along its elusive nuance of bergamot oil.

Setting up our bento, we opposed round and square, flat and concave vessels. And we ranged widely in our selection of dishes, finding an alabaster-like bowl that echoed the translucence of leeks and cheese shavings, a pressed wooden bowl for the grainy rice, a snowy platform of heavily glazed ceramic for the salmon, and a stark slab of travertine—an elegant platform to show off the lamb chop.

Curried Basmati Rice with Raisins

Makes 4 bento servings

2 cups basmati rice

2 cups water

2 teaspoons loose Earl Grey tea (or 1 Earl Grey tea bag)

¼ cup dark raisins

1 tablespoon butter

2 tablespoons mild curry powder

1½ teaspoons kosher salt

Freshly ground black pepper

Wash the rice until the water runs clear. Let the rice soak in the 2 cups of water for 30 minutes.

Make the Earl Grey tea with 1 cup of barely boiling water and let it brew for 4 minutes. Strain the tea onto the raisins in a bowl and let them plump up for 15 minutes.

Melt the butter in a small saucepan with a lid over medium heat and stir in the curry powder. Stir the curry for a few seconds until it starts to color. Stop the curry from cooking by pouring in the rice and water and then add the raisins and salt.

Bring the rice to a boil and stir well. Cover the pot and simmer over low heat for 11 minutes. Remove the pot from the heat and let sit for 5 minutes. Fluff the rice with a fork and season with salt and freshly ground pepper to taste.

Salt-Cured Salmon with Fennel Salad

1 pound kosher salt

⅓ cup whole black peppercorns, cracked in a blender

⅓ cup coriander seeds, cracked in a blender

2 ounces chives, finely sliced

12 ounces salmon fillet cut from the thick part of the fish

1 bulb young fennel

1 tablespoon extra-virgin olive oil

½ tablespoon champagne vinegar or good-quality white wine vinegar

Salt and freshly ground black pepper

In a bowl, mix together the kosher salt, peppercorns, coriander seeds, and chives. Place half of this in a stainless steel, ceramic, or glass baking dish, add the salmon, and cover with the rest of the mixture. Tightly cover the dish with plastic wrap. Let the salmon cure in the refrigerator for 6 hours, then thoroughly brush off the salt and seeds. Slice the salmon very thinly with a clean, sharp, wet knife.

Using a mandoline or sharp knife, slice the fennel very thinly across the grain. Toss the fennel with the olive oil and vinegar and season to taste with salt and pepper. Serve slices of the cured salmon on the fennel salad and garnish with fennel sprigs.

Braised Leeks with Pecorino Cheese

Makes 4 bento servings

1 bunch leeks (4 thick leeks or 6 thin ones), white part and pale green part only

1 tablespoon sweet butter

1 cup chicken stock

Salt and freshly ground black pepper

1 ounce pecorino Romano cheese, shaved in curls from a large piece using a vegetable peeler

Cut the leeks into 1-inch pieces on an angle. Wash the leeks very well, taking care to rid them of any sand. Drain well.

Heat the butter in a small saucepan over medium heat. When the butter is melted, stir in the leeks. Add the chicken stock, season with salt and pepper, and bring to a simmer. Cover the leeks and turn the heat down to low. Cook the leeks at a simmer for 10 minutes, then check for doneness. They should be still firm but not crisp. Let the leeks cool to room temperature in the cooking liquid, then drain well. Serve and garnish with the cheese curls.

Rack of Lamb with
Sweet Mustard Glaze

2 tablespoons sugar

3 tablespoons Dijon mustard

½ New Zealand rack of lamb, with 8 bones, in one piece (have your butcher French
the bones for you)

Salt and freshly ground black pepper

Preheat the oven to 475°F. In a bowl, mix the sugar with the mustard.

Bring the lamb rack to room temperature, leaving it out for up to 1 hour. Season the
rack with salt and pepper and spread the mustard and sugar mix on the surface. Roast the
rack in the hot oven for 10 minutes, remove from the heat, and let rest for 10 minutes. Carve
the rack into 8 chops and serve 2 chops per person.

Winter

*S*pinach with Sesame Seeds

*G*rilled Ham and Cheese Sandwich

*H*erb-Steamed Swordfish

*R*oasted Red Pepper and
Sun-dried Tomato Soup

C an a lunchtime soup and sandwich—a tonic on a winter day—be transformed into an elegant repast? This bento shows how easily everyday foods can be elevated to a new level of sophistication, with the careful execution of a few cooking and presentation techniques.

Here, we've brought a grown-up aesthetic to one of our favorite childhood combinations—tomato soup and a grilled cheese sandwich. The soothing comfort of this simple meal is still there, but the culinary context is made more interesting through new and different ingredients and accompanying dishes our mothers never served us: sun-dried tomatoes, roasted red peppers, a sprightly dish of spinach with a Japanese accent, and a clever second "sandwich" of swordfish stuffed with fresh herbs.

Our grilled ham and cheese sandwich is classic but the pyramidal presentation literally elevates it into a different context. The soup is also utterly simple: sun-dried and fresh tomatoes and roasted red bell peppers are simmered in chicken stock, puréed, and served hot or warm. (The basil garnish is also something that canned soup never enjoys.)

We have balanced the round flavors of the soup and sandwich with the slight astringency of fresh spinach, heated just to wilt, and then lightly dressed with soy sauce and sesame oil and sesame seeds. Though this was not part of our childhood lunches, we have found that kids actually love spinach this way—it is a beautiful glistening green with the nuttiness of sesame seeds.

The second sandwich in this bento is a quick and tempting presentation of swordfish you will want to use on many occasions. A thick fillet is cut in half, filled with fresh dill, tarragon, and parsley, wrapped in plastic wrap, and then steamed for just a few minutes. The flavorful and aromatic package cooks in its own essences and adds a rich and luxurious flavor as well as an exciting visual component to the bento.

Spinach with Sesame Seeds

Makes 4 bento servings

2 bunches spinach, about 2 pounds, stems removed, washed well and spun dry in a
  salad spinner

2 tablespoons sesame oil

1 teaspoon sugar

2 tablespoons soy sauce

1 tablespoon toasted sesame seeds to sprinkle on top of the spinach (see Note)

Heat a sauté pan over medium heat. Add the spinach, sesame oil, sugar, and soy sauce. Cook the spinach, stirring, until the leaves are just wilted, about 3 minutes. Spread the spinach out flat on a plate to cool quickly in the refrigerator for 10 minutes. This will keep the color a vivid green.

When the spinach is cool, taste and correct the seasoning. Pile in a bowl and sprinkle on the toasted sesame seeds. The spinach is served cold.

N O T E   Toast the sesame seeds in a deep frying pan over medium heat, stirring constantly, for about 4 minutes, or until golden brown.

Grilled Ham and Cheese Sandwich

6 slices firm, thinly sliced close-textured white bread, such as Pepperidge Farm

3 tablespoons sweet butter, softened

3 thin slices honey-cured ham

¼ pound sliced Gruyère cheese, white cheddar, Swiss, or other medium-firm cheese

To assemble the sandwiches, butter both sides of each slice of bread. Then lay the ham and cheese on one slice and cover with a second slice of bread. Trim the crusts off the sides of the sandwiches.

Heat a sauté pan over medium-low heat, then fry the sandwiches until the cheese starts to melt and the sandwiches are golden brown, about 3 minutes on each side. You may need to add more butter to the pan.

Remove the sandwiches to paper towels to drain, let them cool for 1 minute, then cut into quarters diagonally and serve 3 quarters each per serving.

Herb-Steamed Swordfish

Makes 4 bento servings

¾ pound swordfish fillet

Salt and freshly ground black pepper

3 tablespoons each of chopped tarragon, dill, and flat-leaf parsley

Sprigs of tarragon, dill, and flat-leaf parsley, for garnish

Cut the swordfish in half horizontally. Season the inside with salt and pepper and fill the center with the chopped herbs. Reassemble the swordfish and season the outside with salt and pepper to taste. Wrap in plastic wrap.

Steam the swordfish in an 8-inch, flat-bottomed steamer, covered, for 6 minutes, or until it is barely opaque.

ASSEMBLY

Remove the plastic wrap. Use a very sharp knife to cut the fish into eight 2-inch wedges. Choose a flat, colorful plate to set off the dramatic form of the fish. Stand one wedge on its end and show the herb filling of the other piece. Garnish with the fresh herbs.

Roasted Red Pepper and Sun-dried Tomato Soup

Makes 4 bento servings

1 ounce sun-dried tomatoes (about 8 pieces—do not use the oil-packed type)

1 small onion, diced

2 tablespoons extra-virgin olive oil

2 cups chicken stock

3 sweet or bell red peppers, charred, skinned, and seeded (see page 145), or a 6-ounce jar of prepared roasted sweet peppers

2 fresh ripe plum tomatoes, cut into eighths

Salt and freshly ground black pepper to taste

4 fresh basil leaves, for garnish (use purple basil if available)

Rehydrate the dried tomatoes by soaking them in warm water for 1 hour.

Sweat the onion in the olive oil in a 2-quart saucepan over medium heat, uncovered, for 7 to 10 minutes, stirring occasionally. Do not let the onion color.

Add the stock, rehydrated tomatoes, roasted peppers, fresh tomatoes, salt, and pepper and let it all simmer together for 10 minutes.

Pour the soup into a blender and process at high speed for 4 minutes, until very smooth. Then pass it through a strainer to remove the vegetable skins. Adjust the seasoning and serve with fresh basil leaves as a garnish.

Grilled Fennel Sausage
with Stewed Onions

Crispy Vegetable Chips

Fried Catfish in Cornmeal Crust

Ellen's Pickled Vegetables

In this delicious bento, visual composition and flavor enjoy the same play of "shapes." The thin clear lines of a sharp triangular vessel—full of colorful wedges and pyramids of pickled vegetables—provides a dynamic counterpoint to the round, soft-edged, and muted dishes that surround it. And similarly, the sharp and refreshing flavor of the pickles provides a sparkling foil to the rich, round, and sweet tastes of deep-fried catfish, vegetable chips, grilled sausage, and wine-infused onions.

Once again, the bento frame works a kind of magic on humble, homey, and satisfying food: fish and chips and sausage with onion. Carefully prepared food proves beautiful itself and a gorgeous presentation doesn't demand much more than attentive slicing and frying.

You can start this meal a day ahead, making the deep-fried root vegetable chips. Thin slicing—very thin—is a must and you will want to use a French or Japanese mandoline. The parsnip slices, with their hard core and soft edges, crisp into a beautiful ruffled shape. All the chips—parsnip, russet, and sweet potato—are irresistibly salty and sweet: The hardest part will be saving enough for your bento meal.

We understand why fried catfish is such a popular American favorite. Widely available and reasonably priced, it yields a golden crust and sweet, succulent interior—when it is cooked properly. You can save and reuse the oil from frying the chips, but you will want to fry the catfish at a higher temperature—and at the last minute before serving the meal.

We add a couple of special touches to the sausage and onions, giving this time-honored combination a striking intensity of flavor and a deep color. If possible, find thin Italian luganega sausage, with fennel seed. The proportions of this thin sausage match the bento, and they should be sliced in small angular pieces. The red onions gain a remarkable sweetness and rich color from a slow simmer with a whole bottle of red wine. Our recipe will yield a good supply of this marvelous condiment, which will keep well for weeks and add flavor to myriad dishes.

The sharp, clean look of the pickled carrot, red and yellow bell pepper, and daikon radish is enhanced by careful slicing. Use a roll cut on the carrots and daikon and cut the peppers into sharp-cornered triangles. Their appearance will be well matched to their sweet and sharp taste. Just an hour in sushi su—a simple mixture of rice vinegar, sugar, and salt—will produce a wonderful and brightly flavored pickle. Be sure to use daikon if you can find it: Its mustardlike tang adds immeasurably to the pleasure of this dish.

Grilled Fennel Sausage
with Stewed Onions

Makes 4 bento servings

4 medium red onions, sliced ¼ inch thick

1 clove garlic, crushed and minced

3 tablespoons extra-virgin olive oil

1 bottle full-flavored red wine, not acidic, such as a cabernet sauvignon, pinot noir, or merlot

1 pound fresh, thin sweet Italian sausage, such as luganega

Salt and freshly ground black pepper

Sprigs of watercress

Preheat a charcoal or stove-top grill.

In a small pot over medium-low heat, sweat the onions and the garlic in the oil, uncovered, for 10 to 12 minutes, until softened but not browned.

Add the wine and cook, stirring occasionally, until the onions are very soft and the wine has evaporated, about 30 minutes.

Meanwhile, grill the sausage for 15 minutes, with salt and freshly ground pepper to taste, or until done. Let the sausage rest for 10 minutes before slicing. Serve the sausage pieces over the onion mix and garnish with a few sprigs of watercress.

Crispy Vegetable Chips

Makes 4 bento servings

1 medium russet baking potato, peeled

1 sweet potato, peeled

2 large parsnips, peeled

2 quarts peanut or canola oil

Salt

Use a French or Japanese mandoline to cut ¹⁄₁₆-inch or thinner slices of the root vegetables. Cut as thinly as possible. Keep each vegetable separate.

Heat the oil in a deep 8-quart pot to 330°F. (A thermometer will be helpful for this.)

Fry each root vegetable in small batches until lightly browned. Remove to paper towels to drain and lightly salt immediately. Let the chips crisp and cool for 10 minutes and then serve. Pile the chips up, alternating different types.

Fried Catfish in Cornmeal Crust

1 quart peanut or canola oil

¾ pound catfish fillet, cut into 4 even pieces

Salt and freshly ground black pepper

1 cup all-purpose flour

1 egg, lightly beaten

1 cup medium ground yellow or white cornmeal

In a 4-quart pot, heat the oil to 350°F. (A thermometer will be helpful for this.)

Season both sides of the fish with salt and pepper. Dredge the fillets in the flour. Coat each piece evenly and shake off any excess flour. Dip the fillets into the egg and then dredge in the cornmeal.

Fry the catfish in the oil for 5 to 6 minutes, or until the crust is golden brown. Do this in 2 batches. Drain the catfish on paper towels. Serve while still hot.

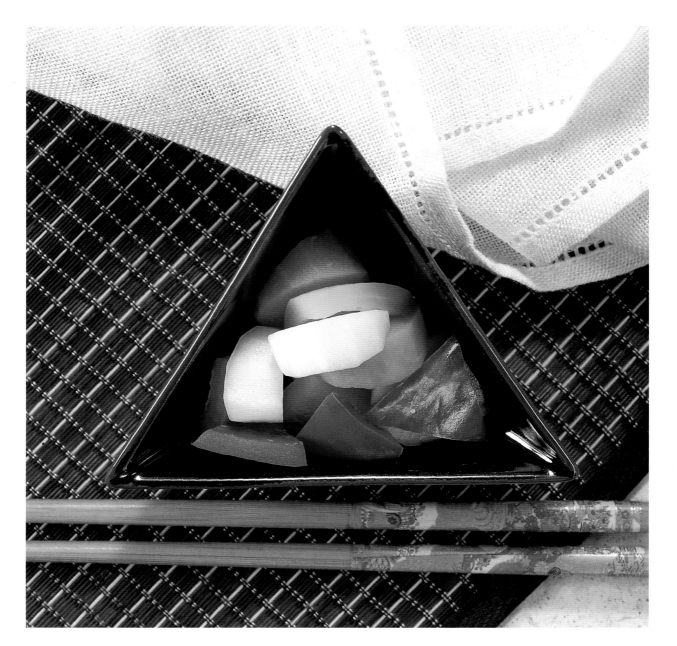

Ellen's Pickled Vegetables

Makes 4 bento servings

1 cup rice vinegar

¼ cup sugar

3 tablespoons salt

¼ cup water

1 carrot, peeled and roll cut into ½-inch pieces

1 red bell pepper, cut into ½-inch triangles

1 yellow bell pepper, cut into ½-inch triangles

½ daikon radish (or substitute 1 bunch red radishes if daikon radish is not available), peeled and roll cut into ½-inch pieces

In a small saucepan, heat the rice vinegar, sugar, salt, and water over medium heat until the sugar and salt dissolve, approximately 3 to 4 minutes. Pour the hot mixture over the vegetable pieces in a nonreactive bowl and let sit for 1 hour at room temperature or 4 hours in the refrigerator. Serve cold or at room temperature.

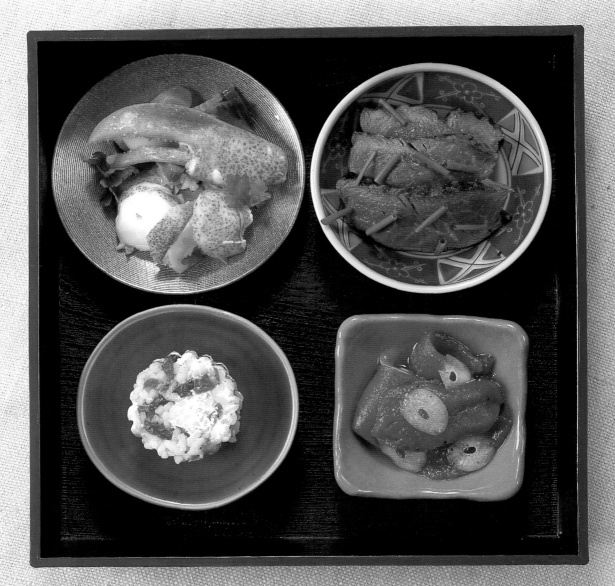

Roasted Red Peppers
with Olive Oil and Vinegar

Lobster on Leeks with Fennel and Carrot

Rare Filet Mignon

Arborio Rice with Goat Cheese and Tomato

This is our "champagne" bento—a menu of pure luxury, perfect for an elegant and intimate celebration (think New Year's Eve). The lush display of lobster and filet mignon together is a sensual thrill for every guest—and here we have heightened the sense of extravagance with a dramatic golden platter and vibrant tableau of red, green, and blue elements.

As in all our bentos, the essential elegance derives from the simplicity of preparation and presentation. You can buy cooked lobster, but we recommend that you follow our directions, cooking the crustacean in water with the salinity of the ocean. The meat will be the most succulent you have ever tasted. We embellish the dish with a sweet mix of braised aromatic vegetables—leeks, fennel, and carrots—which lend the perfume of a court bouillon. Display the lobster atop the vegetables: There is no culinary shape as tempting and evocative as a whole claw of lobster meat (and we give clear instructions for removing it intact from the shell).

It is even easier to get the pure and luscious flavor of rare filet mignon. Allow the meat to reach room temperature and sauté for 3 minutes on each side, with a touch of olive oil. Slice and sprinkle with chives.

Though the accompaniments we present are less expensive than the meats, they are just as luscious in the mouth. Arborio rice is cooked as for a risotto, its creaminess enhanced with goat cheese. Flecks of plumped sun-dried tomato add savor and color. A mild tang and more sweet succulence is provided by the slices of roasted red pepper, briefly marinated with balsamic vinegar, salt, pepper, and paper-thin slices of garlic.

This is, of course, a meal to be served on the most elegant dishes that your bento will accommodate. As can be seen, we literally "pulled out all the stops" in assembling our box. We were so enamored of the slightly oversized, ridged, gold platter on which we serve the lobster that we removed the bento's crosspieces to give it the space it deserves. This is one meal where you can't get too much of all the good things.

Roasted Red Peppers
with Olive Oil and Vinegar

Makes 4 bento servings

4 fresh sweet red bell peppers or a 6-ounce jar of prepared roasted sweet peppers

1 tablespoon balsamic vinegar

2 cloves garlic, sliced very fine

Salt and freshly ground black pepper

2 tablespoons extra-virgin olive oil

If using fresh peppers, roast the red peppers over a gas flame until the skin blackens and blisters. Alternatively, you can do this in a very hot, 500°F oven. Place the peppers in a paper bag to cool and loosen their skins. Then slip the skins off with a damp towel or scrape them off with a dull knife while the peppers are still warm. Remove the seeds and cut the flesh into serving pieces.

Toss the peppers with the vinegar first, then the garlic. Add salt and pepper to taste and finally the olive oil. Toss together again.

Let marinate 1 hour or longer before serving.

Lobster on Leeks with Fennel and Carrot

Makes 4 bento servings

3 tablespoons chopped shallot

1 teaspoon butter

1 tablespoon olive oil

2 leeks, washed and sliced into ¼-inch slices

1 small fennel bulb, cut into ¼-inch slices

1 medium carrot, peeled and cut into ¼-inch rounds

¼ cup chicken stock

¼ cup vermouth

Salt and freshly ground black pepper

2 live lobsters, 1½ pounds each, or 10 ounces of lobster meat

Sprigs of fresh flat-leaf parsley or chervil

In a saucepan over medium-low heat, sweat the shallot in the butter and oil until soft. Add the leeks, fennel, carrot, chicken stock, and vermouth and season with salt and pepper. Cover with a tight-fitting lid and let simmer over medium heat for 10 minutes, or until soft.

If using live lobsters, boil a large pot of water with enough salt so that it is as salty as sea-water. Separate the lobster claws, with the elbows attached, from the body. Pull the tails from the bodies and insert a skewer between the shell and the meat on the underside to keep the tail straight. Cook the claws in the boiling salted water for 4 minutes. Add the tails to the pot and continue to cook for another 6 minutes. Cool the cooked claws and tails in iced, salted water.

Once the lobsters have cooled, remove the meat from the shells. Use a heavy towel to protect your hands. Bend the elbows close to the claw and cut off the outer ¼ inch of shell.

Open up the elbow and gently pull out the meat. Bend the movable pincer backward until it cracks, wiggle it from side to side to loosen it from the main claw, then gently pull it away from the claw. Use the back of a heavy knife to crack the claw shell. Go around the entire claw, pull the shell apart, and remove the claw meat in one piece. To remove the tail meat from the shell, just wrap it with the towel and squeeze the sides together until you hear a crack as the underside of the shell breaks. Hook your thumbs under the bottom sides of the shell and pry it apart. Gently pull out the tail meat.

Serve the lobster on the vegetables and garnish with flat-leaf parsley or chervil.

NOTE ON USING LIVE LOBSTERS We use the above technique in our restaurant kitchens for more precise cooking of the lobsters. As the claws take longer to cook than the tails, it makes sense to separate the lobster's body parts before cooking. However, if you don't desire to do this, simply plunge the whole lobster into boiling salted water and cook for 10 minutes. Cool and remove the meat from the shells as directed.

Rare Filet Mignon

Makes 4 bento servings

1 pound filet mignon, completely trimmed by your butcher

Salt and freshly ground black pepper

3 tablespoons extra-virgin olive oil

1 tablespoon chives, cut into ½-inch-long pieces

Let the meat come to room temperature before cooking, up to 1 hour. Heat a small sauté pan over medium heat. Pat the meat dry with a clean towel. Season to taste with salt and pepper. Put the oil in the pan and sear the filet for 5 minutes on each side. Let the meat rest for 10 minutes, then slice with a very sharp knife. Serve with the cut chives as a garnish.

Arborio Rice with Goat Cheese and Tomato

6 pieces sun-dried tomato, rehydrated for 15 minutes in warm water

1 cup Arborio rice (a short-grain Italian rice)

1 tablespoon extra-virgin olive oil

2 cups boiling chicken stock

2 ounces fresh, semisoft goat cheese

Salt and freshly ground black pepper

Chop the rehydrated tomato into pieces the size of peas.

Stir the rice with the olive oil in a 1-quart pot over medium heat for 2 minutes. While stirring the rice, add the boiling stock, ½ cup at a time. When all of the liquid is added, the rice should be creamy, with some resistance.

Let the rice cool for 5 minutes, then stir in the cheese and tomato and season with salt and pepper to taste. Press in a rice press or shape by hand. We pressed this rice in a crenellated cookie cutter. Serve warm.

Sources for Bento Boxes

The following sources are listed for purchasing bento boxes of all types, including shokado bentos. At these stores you will also find porcelain, glass, and lacquer dishes of various sizes and styles. You may also find foodstuffs and kitchenware, such as rice presses and molds. Just inquire at the stores nearest you.

Takashimaya New York
693 Fifth Avenue
New York, NY 10022
(212) 350-0100
(800) 753-2038
Takashimaya sells shokado bento boxes with lids and with selected dishes to go in the compartments. The boxes and rice presses are available through mail order.

Katagiri Seikatsukan Inc.
224 East 59th Street
New York, NY 10022
(212) 755-3566

Utsuwa No Yakata
(five locations)
(800) 269-5099
508 Mamaroneck Avenue
White Plains, NY 10605
(914) 289-0790

Yao Han Plaza
595 River Road
Edgewater, NJ 07020
(201) 941-9113

544 10th Street
Palisades Park, NJ 07650
(201) 346-0032

100 Algonquin Road
Arlington Heights, IL 60005
(847) 640-0820

333 South Alameda Street
Los Angeles, CA 90013
(213) 621-2071

Kam Kuo Food Corporation
7 Mott Street
New York, NY 10013
(212) 349-3097

Index

Page numbers in *italics* refer to bento box menus.

cheese (continued)

    braised leeks with
        pecorino, *109–110*, 114
    butternut squash soup with
        Parmesan, *97–99*, 101
    mozzarella and anchovy
        salad, focaccia with,
        35–36, 43
    sandwich, grilled ham and,
        121–122, 125

chicken:

    breast with corn, walnuts,
        and cilantro, *47–49*, 51
    Japanese rice with soy glaze
        and, *97–99*, 102
    nuggets with spicy
        cucumber, *59–61*, 63

chips, crispy vegetable,
    131–133, 136

chives, Japanese rice with
    hard-boiled eggs and,
    11–13, 19–20

cilantro, chicken breast with
    corn, walnuts, and,
    47–49, 51

cod, braised, with green
    beans, cranberry beans,
    and flat beans, *59–61*,
    68–69

coriander, baby artichokes
    with thyme and, *11–13*,
    18

corn:

    chicken breast with
        walnuts, cilantro and,
        47–49, 51

    scallops and mussels with
        orzo, tomato and,
        71–72, 73–75

Cornish hen, roast, *11–13*, 15

cornmeal crust, fried catfish
    in, *131–133*, 138

crabs, soft-shell, tempura, on
    spicy watercress, *97–99*,
    105–106

cranberry beans, braised cod
    with green beans, flat
    beans and, *59–61*,
    68–69

cucumber, chicken nuggets
    with spicy, *59–61*, 63

curried:

    acorn squash with pecans,
        59–61, 64
    basmati rice with raisins,
        109–110, 111

D

daikon radish in Ellen's
    pickled vegetables,
    131–133, 141

E

eggplant in ratatouille, *85–87*,
    90–92

eggs, hard-boiled, Japanese
    rice with chives and,
    11–13, 19–20

F

fennel:

    lobster on leeks with carrot
        and, *143–144*, 147–148
    salad, salt-cured salmon
        with, *109–110*, 113
    sausage, grilled, with stewed
        onions, *131–133*, 135

filet mignon, rare, *143–144*,
    148

fish:

    braised cod with green beans,
        cranberry beans, and flat
        beans, *59–61*, 68–69
    fried catfish in cornmeal
        crust, *131–133*, 138
    herb-steamed swordfish,
        121–122, 126
    salt-cured salmon with fen-
        nel salad, *109–110*, 113
    seared salmon on Napa
        cabbage, *23–25*, 30
    seared tuna with sesame
        seed crust and caramel
        soy, *47–49*, 55–56

focaccia with mozzarella and
    anchovy salad, *35–36*, 43

G

garlic:

    in baby artichokes with
        coriander and thyme,
        11–13, 18

Index

154

soup:

    butternut squash, with
        Parmesan, *97–99*, 101

    roasted red pepper and
        sun-dried tomato,
        121–122, 129

    sweet and snow pea, *71–72*,
        76

sources for bento boxes, 152

soy:

    caramel, seared tuna with
        sesame seed crust and,
        47–49, *55–56*

    glaze, Japanese rice with
        chicken and, *97–99*, 102

    sauce and sake marinade,
        grilled quail in, *35–36*,
        37–38

    sauce in grilled steak with
        red onions, *71–72*,
        81–82

spinach with sesame seeds,
    121–122, 123

steak, grilled, with red onions,
    71–72, 81–82

sweet potato in crispy vegetable
    chips, *131–133*, 136

swordfish, herb-steamed,
    121–122, 126

T

tempura soft-shell crabs on
    spicy watercress, *97–99*,
    105–106

thyme, baby artichokes with
    coriander and, *11–13*, 18

tomato(es):

    Arborio rice with goat
        cheese and, *143–144*, 151

    and bread salad, *47–49*, 57

    in ratatouille, *85–87*,
        90–92

    roasted, in tempura
        soft-shell crabs on spicy
        watercress, *97–99*,
        105–106

    salad of shrimp with
        chanterelles and, *35–36*,
        40

    sauce, raw, pasta with,
        85–87, 92

    scallops and mussels
        with corn, orzo, and,
        71–72, *73–75*

    sun-dried, and roasted red
        pepper soup, *121–122*,
        129

    sun-dried, Japanese rice with
        bacon and, *47–49*, 52

tuna, seared, with sesame seed
    crust and caramel soy,
    47–49, *55–56*

V

vegetable(s):

    chips, crispy, *131–133*, 136

    Ellen's pickled, *131–133*,
    141

vinegar, roasted red peppers
    with olive oil and,
    143–144, 145

W

walnuts:

    chicken breast with corn,
        cilantro and, *47–49*,
        51

    potato salad with olives
        and, *11–13*, 16

watercress, tempura soft-shell
    crabs on spicy, *97–99*,
    105–106

wild rice with pine nuts and
    sweet peas, *35–36*,
    44

wine, red, in grilled fennel
    sausage with stewed
    onions, *131–133*,
    135

Y

yellow summer squash in
    ratatouille, *85–87*,
    90–92

Z

zucchini in ratatouille, *85–87*,
    90–92